THE PORCUPINE HUNTER

THE PORCUPINE HUNTER
AND OTHER STORIES:
THE ORIGINAL TSIMSHIAN TEXTS
OF HENRY W. TATE

newly transcribed
from the original manuscripts
and annotated
by
Ralph Maud

Talonbooks   Vancouver   1993

Copyright © 1993 Ralph Maud

Published with assistance from the Canada Council

Talonbooks
201 - 1019 East Cordova
Vancouver, British Columbia
Canada V6A 1M8

Typeset in Garamond by Pièce de Résistance Ltée., and printed and bound in Canada by Hignell Printing Ltd.

First Printing: October 1993

Canadian Cataloguing in Publication Data

Tate, Henry W.
  The porcupine hunter and other stories

  ISBN 0-88922-333-5

  1. Tsimshian Indians—Legends. 2. Indians of North America—British Columbia—Legends. I. Maud, Ralph, 1928- II. Title.
E99.T8T37 1993   398.2'08'9979   C93-091806-1

CONTENTS

Introduction

Fort Simpson, later Port Simpson, near the present-day Prince Rupert, B.C., was named after the Hudson Bay's chief trader on the Pacific coast, Aemilius Simpson. By the time of Henry Tate's birth there, it was an "old" establishment of a quarter of a century's trading, and had long been a focus of activity for many of the Tsimshian tribes of the Skeena River, who lived part of the year around the stockade in large rectangular cedar-plank houses.

We can only guess at Tate's birth date. He was probably still a teenager at the time of William Ridley's arrival from the Punjab in 1879 to take over the duties of Bishop of Caledonia. Tate must have worked with Ridley for some years on the translation of the Gospels into Tsimshian prior to its publication in 1886, for his subsequent work for Franz Boas shows that he had learnt the Ridley orthography very thoroughly. "No missionary can be dull among the Zimshian Indians," wrote the good Bishop in his *Snapshots from the North Pacific* (London 1903). "They have an alertness of mind and purpose which forbids stagnation." He must have had someone in mind when he said this, and it could have been Henry W. Tate.

Tate's middle initial stands for "Wellington"—a name that was possibly acquired at the time of his adoption by Arthur Wellington (Clah), when he was given the status of "sister's son" within the matrilinear system of the Tsimshians. We know about the adoption because Boas mentions it in the notes to *Tsimshian Mythology* (1916:500). Its significance lies in the sequence of events which produced from Henry Tate's pen the Tsimshian texts of that massive volume. George Hunt, Boas's trusted Kwakiutl informant, told Boas that if he wanted Tsimshian history and lore he should contact Arthur Wellington (Clah). Hunt was right that Clah was the most notable and verbal of living Tsimshian, but he was quite wrong to think that Clah would or could cooperate in writing down Tsimshian myths on paper. What we have of Clah's manuscripts shows not only a great difficulty with English constructions but also a total commitment to furthering the missionary work of the inspired William Duncan. When Clah received Boas's letter of

15 April 1903 he was probably about to go off to do some lay preaching somewhere, to eradicate heathen thoughts from the minds of the populace. Fortunately, he did not tear up Boas's letter: he handed it to Henry Tate.

We would know a good deal more about Tate if his first letter, introducing himself to Boas, were extant. As it is, we know hardly anything about him except that, like everybody else, he went up to the Nass every year for the olachen run and did his summer fishing, and that, unlike anybody else, he could write a good clear Tsimshian story in passable English. In the ten years from 1903 until his death in 1913, he mailed to Boas in New York about two thousand pages of interlinear text in English and Tsimshian, a most impressive achievement. Even William Beynon, who does not praise easily, told Marius Barbeau that Tate "did not have the full confidence of all his informants...nor money to pay them. In spite of that he seems to have done well" (letter of 19 March 1918).

Beynon stresses an important point. Tate was not given money by Boas for informants; he was paid by the page. So he wrote. And who knows how much of what he wrote came out of his own creative talent? Boas does not entertain the possibility that Tate can be anything more than a transmitter of tribal knowledge; and when he publishes the stories, first in *Tsimshian Texts* (1912) and then in the "monumental" *Tsimshian Mythology* (1916) Boas seems only concerned to enter them as raw data for an extensive analysis of myth motifs and culture. A more broadly appreciative view seems called for. Indeed, the reason for the present volume is the acute dissatisfaction one experiences with Boas's published texts after one has seen Tate's actual manuscript pages.[1] They are much more vivid and engaging than the normalization to standard English in the fare Boas has offered us. Although there are questions of accuracy and distortion that arise in connection with Boas's methodology, this edition is not concerned with detailing previous error, but with simply freeing Tate from the previous restraint. The aim is to present the interested reader with the best of Tate's texts as found in the original manuscripts, with all their attractive spontaneity, the unpremeditated writing of someone from an oral tradition diving headlong into a new written medium.

The curious thing is that, while Tate obviously spoke and thought in Tsimshian and therefore had these stories in his head in his native language, when he came to write them down for Boas, he wrote them in English first, then supplied the Tsimshian equivalent interlinearly afterwards. This is perfectly clear from a perusal of the documents. Once Boas realized what Tate was doing, he asked him not to (letters of 22 May 1905 and 26 September 1905). Boas wanted the Tsimshian to be the primary text, but Tate, for whatever reason, continued writing the English first as before. So Boas had to make do. Boas's loss is our gain, because we have these stories as English compositions, not as translations.[2]

The editor asks the reader's trust in the validity of the editorial decisions that produced the final form of the texts on the following pages. There has been a small amount of correction of spelling, punctuation, and grammar. A very small amount. How little has been emended will appear from the myriad non-standard constructions deliberately left in the narratives. If some, why were there not more changes made? It seemed that the quick life of the pieces was contained in the precise actual phrasing, which was not to be disturbed except to avoid something *very* confusing. Tate's unusual diction was interesting and valuable, but fidelity to mere scribal errors would be misplaced. The aim was to leave Tate's idiosyncrasies substantially intact, while silently caring to adjust what was too annoying. The reader should trust that there is not a word in these pages that is not Tate's—there may be plenty of punctuation and capital letters that are not.

There is another motive besides "quaintness" for leaving Tate's sentences awkward, if they are. It slows down the reading. These stories told in the traditional fireside setting were enunciated deliberately, with emphatic pauses. There was no rush. If the "substandard" grammar makes it difficult for the reader to skim along the surface of these texts, then all to the good. The editor has shaped the text on the page to the same end: to suggest by means of the white spaces that an important part of the story's value is in its unhurried pace.[3] Tate does not himself provide any paragraphing; he cannot imagine that we will not know how to obey the movement of the narrative. How can the printed page offer the story a proper telling? How can it give the story time to sink in? To somehow interrupt the normal flow of the line is perhaps the only way. White space. Plus the use of italics for those sentences or paragraphs where Tate is standing outside his story and commenting on it.

One other thing: Tate's titles are sometimes very curious. The editor has provided an additional title for each of the stories, for convenience and in some cases to reflect more accurately what seems to be the focus of the tale. The editor has also attempted to group the stories into appropriate genre types, as a way of intimating to the reader the broad intention behind a story. The head-notes and footnotes may provide some useful information, but they are mainly a way of indicating one reader's appreciation of Tate's achievement.

The above summarizes the extent of the interference with the text. The editor has otherwise not come between Tate and his readers. Here are the best of his stories[4] as he wrote them in his corner of Port Simpson, B.C.

Ralph Maud

Notes

1 Columbia University Special Collections Library has the great majority of the extant Tate manuscripts, with just one story manuscript each at the American Philosophical Society, Philadelphia, and the Smithsonian Institution, Washington, D.C. The editor acknowledges indebtedness to these institutions for access to the Tate collections and for permission to publish: "The Deserted Youth" from the American Philosophical Society, "Son, Moon, and Fog" from the Smithsonian, and the remainder from Columbia.

2 This means that the editor, who is not a linguist, can presume to present them in their most authentic form, which is English. The Tsimshian line has not, however, been ignored; and help was gratefully received from experts in the field, John A. Dunn and Margaret Seguin.

3 Although the editor has appreciated very much the work of Dell Hymes in revealing the prosodic structure of story-tellings, the lay-out of the Tate stories here is not Hymesian. Hymes's book, *"In Vain I Tried To Tell You"* (1981) shows that linguistic markers inherent in all languages are signposts that allow for stories that would normally appear as blocks of prose to be arranged with more fidelity as verse lines; but the method requires such expertise in languages and such persistence in analysis that we can expect to see in this form only fairly short pieces done by a limited number of scholars. The editor's arrangement of Tate's text on these pages is merely an instinctive response to perceived dramatic requirements within the text.

4 It is unfortunate that, after the publication of *Tsimshian Mythology* (1916), several hundred pages of the Tate manuscripts were separated from the collection, and are missing. Some of Tate's best work was therefore not available for this edition.

ANIMALS AND HUMANS

The Porcupine Hunter

The porcupines have decided to impose their own ecological rules of game management. This hunter is getting entirely too rich through mass marketing of porcupine meat. "Don't kill so many." The point is driven home by a nightmare—a product of the hunter's uneasy conscience, if you will. It is quilled into him.

As a matter of fact, good authority has it that, despite popular lore, porcupines cannot throw their quills. The hunter's face would only get pincushioned if he were shortsighted and had to peer at a porcupine closely. Then indeed he would need a miracle ointment, for the quills have teeth that make it almost impossible to draw them from flesh. Much of the passion of this story is in the irrepressible desire of the narrator to tell the good news about the antidote—which would seem, however, to have its olfactory downside. Not to forget the freshly chewed greenery for the complexion. And don't eat young porcupine heads. Oh, the story is full of good advice.

The advice seems to be the essence of the matter. The plot is not one that is well-known on the coast; in fact, there are no analogues recorded. Nevertheless, there are archaic elements: for instance, the porcupine's song. Songs in stories are never recent compositions; and this one no doubt belonged originally in another setting, for the song concerns *pronouncing* the name not guessing it. It is the sort of chant that would accompany a shibboleth test. In a war situation, this weeds out friend from foe. The Ephraimites could pronounce the word only as "sibboleth"; the Bible tells that 42,000 failed the test.

In this story the test is a way of going through what are presumably common nicknames for Porcupine, ending with a rehabilitation of his chiefly name. The hunter will have to fail, up to a point, in order to be saved by the archetypal friendly animal, Mouse Woman, as so many lost souls in these stories are. For the wrong answer he gets quill on his face. The story-teller can then give us the healing recipe.

The story of Porcupine Hunter

There was a great Porcupine hunter in one of the native Village. Every year he went in the early Fall to hunt some Porcupine, it because their are a rich food in those days among the natives. Every Fall he has slain so many and dried their meats and fats, and in the Winter time some stranges people from different Villages come to him and buy the dried meats from him and he became a very rich man. He has many Valleys for his hunting grown, and he has build a huts in each valley to dried meats and tallow in each huts. He has four valleys as his hunting grown. Every year he went to his first camp, and when he slew all the porcupines, then he went to the next camp, then when he slew them all, he went to another camp, and so on. He made a good club of Bow-wood[1] very hart wood, to clubbed the Porcupine. After he made smoke in the den of the Porcupine and when the Porcupine ran out that he clubbed them to slain.

Then all the Porcupine regretful
                              and distress
                                        for this man.

15

Therefore on these last year of this hunter stard very early in than other Fall. That he went to camp on his four camps, and this time he has gain a great number of Porcupine slains. And when he had filled his three huts, then went to the last camp grown too. As he arrived there in the same day

                    that he went alone to looked over the large rock a little further above his huts, and when he reached there, then he saw a large Porcupine

                    a brown fur.

Just went round

        at foot of a large Spruce tree

                that stood at the frount

of rock yonder.

        He ran after it,

           and he behold a large door

                    was

already opened

        before him a large fire burned

                in the centre of a

large house

        who invited him in.

So he enter there and they spread a mats on one side of the fire, and a great chief seated at the real of his house. Then he order to his young men and said, ran around the Village and invite all them women in my house that I might dance to welcome my guest.

    So they went,

        then all them

              women are come in

          and he stood
          the Porcupine
          to dance,
          then the leader
          of the singing
          begun to singing.

And this is their singing: "Pronounce my name, Pronounce my name, strike, strike." This is the words of this tune. Repeat many.

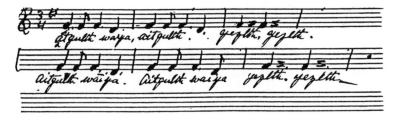

The Porcupine ran
around his own
large fire
and when the singing rest a while that he stood at the frount of his guest and he said to his guest, the hunter, Pronounce my name my brother who is my name says he while he stop and stood before. Then the hunter said thy name is "Little Porcupine." Yes, my name is that, says the chief Porcupine
while he striked
the hunter's face
with his pinne-tail.
They begun to sing again, and the Chief Porcupine begun to dance once more, while the hunter's face was full with the Porcupine pins. And at the end of their singing that he stopped before the hunter and said, Now whose my name my brother said he. Thy name is "Little Ugly Porcupine."

He striked his face again with his pinne-tail and said I that is my name. Then they sing again, the Chief Porcupine ran around the fire while his attendants keep singing, and he stopped again before him. Who is my name my brother? The man said thy name is "Little Scorch."[2] He striked him again with pinne-tail. Yes, that is my name, and the hunter's face full with the pins of Porcupine.

Then his face was swollen
it's very hartly
to see his eyes.
Again the chief Porcupine ran around his fire while they singing. He stop again at before him. Now who is my name my brother? says he. The poor grief hunter said, Thy name is "Little Leaning Fellow." Yes, that is my name, says the Chief Porcupine while he strike his face with his pinne-tail. He ran around again, and his

17

attendants keep singing little longer, for this is the last time of the life of this man.

    That a soft touched

                by his side.

                        It was a Mouse Woman

who asked him, Did you know these who punished you? The poor blind hunter said no. It is the porcupine Chief, said the Mouse Woman, because you slew them every years passed.

    During Porcupine singing

                that the Mouse Woman

                        talk to him.

Now you may be last time at the end of their singing then all these Porcupine will be strike all over your body with their pinne-tails, if you not right answer to the chief's name. His name is "Sea-otter of Green Side Mountain."[3]

    And while the Mouse Woman

                  talk to him

                        their singing was

    ceased.

Then all those Porcupines are ready rush on him. Then the chief at the frount of him and said, Now who is my name dear man? Then the poor man that was blind was answered with his low voice and said, Thy name is "Sea-otter at Green Side of a Mountain."

    Then the Chief Porcupine order his people to wash the face of the poor man. Then all the Porcupine working at this man's face, and they took out the new green excrement[4] from the stomach of the first wife of the chief Porcupine, and they rubbed on his face where the pins was. Then some pins are come out again by itself. Then they took the second wife of the chief excrement they rubbed on his face, and some of the pins came out again, and man's face was become less pins than it was before. Then the thirth wife's excrement they rubbed, and the swell on his face became less, the pins loose and fell off from his face. The fourth wife of the chief excrement are rubbed on his face, and all those pins are all come out, and not one single pins are remain in the face of this hunter. Then the chief Porcupine has chewing the new green leaves, and he spat in his own hands and he rubbed on the face of this man, and the face of the hunter became as beauty as when he was a boy.

Then Chief Porcupine
                    order his attendants
                                        to give him food.
Therefore they brought him a fatting of the mountain sheep meats,
and all different kinds of food, fruits of all kinds. And when the
hunter felt satisfy, after he ate food in the house, then the Chief
have said to him, I will become to you friends together. He said,
My people are much regretfully for you have slew great number of
them. So I took you in to my house to slay you right there. But
because you are right to pronounce my chief name, therefore I'll
save your life.
        Wherefore I ask you kind
                            don't made smoke
                                            in the Den of
Porcupines
            in any places.
                        If you need Porcupine's meat
don't kill so many of them.
                        And soon as you kill one
                                            or more
than that
            dried their meats in good fire,
                                    and finished
to eat them soon
                before winter
so that my people would not had any sickness in the
Winter. And cast   the Porcupine's bones   into fire[5]   and
let not your young people   ate the head of the young
Porcupine   lest they forgot   everything.

*So the natives knew how to use the excrement of the Porcupines
when the Porcupine's pins are stuck in the body of our people.*

Then the hunter went out from there to his own huts, while his
wife sitting there and weeping, because her husband lost many
days. While the woman was sitting there she heard a noise at the
door she turn round her face and look her husband come in, and
she wonderer, and ask him. The hunter told her that he been from
the house of the chief Porcupine. Then they move, and went
home. They took all his slains from the other camps, and when he

took them all down home, he want to invited all the natives to his house and told them what happened to him and how punishment he had in the house of Chief Porcupine

many days.

Therefore people nowadays knew. The Porcupine distress for the people. Porcupine was a singing animals, they knows every tunes of all kind.[6] This the end.

Notes

1 "Bow-wood": yew. Tate's Tsimshian line uses the word for yew tree. Actually, porcupines—so they say—are very easy to kill, which further compounds the hunter's offense: "People who are lost and without weapons have often been saved from starvation by meeting up with a porcupine; consequently, a northern rule of etiquette—observed by both Indians and whites—is that one should not ordinarily kill a porcupine if one has other food" (McClellan 1975:153).

2 "Little Scorch": The hunter probably knew how Porcupine got its scorched back from hearing the well-known story (below) in which Grizzly Bear puts Porcupine through a fire torture. The hunter seems particularly obtuse in thinking that Porcupine would welcome being reminded of this indignity.

3 "Sea-otter": usually considered a malevolent creature. Names are rarely flattering in Tsimshian culture; they often represent a slur that has been lived down, or "bidded up" by potlatch gifts. There is no immediately significant message in this sea-otter name; there is probably a lost pun in the Tsimshian: Gu'lau'um lak shiekshat (Tate's orthography). These are not the usual words for "sea-otter" or "green" or "mountain."

4 "Excrement": "[B]oth the Tagish and Inland Tlingit empty the contents of the porcupine's bladder and stomach onto the quills, since they believe that this helps to work them out" (McClellan 1975:153).

5 "Bones into fire": "Although this is no longer the practice today, older informants recall that animal bones should be burned and should be 'talked' to as they are stirred about in the flames" (Miller and Eastman 1984:9).

6 "Every tunes of all kind": This is the kind of non-sequitor that really authenticates a story. It is an idea that has to have come from the "folk," not from a modern man like Henry Tate.

The Hunter's Wife Changed into a Beaver

We have stories of possession, where animal characteristics insidiously take over the human being. This story might be considered to be such if it were not for a suspicion that the hunter's wife was exercising free choice. She preferred to be a beaver. It is almost as though she had been waiting for an excuse, and her "shame" was being offered to the community as a possibly acceptable motive. Until recently, wives were not supposed to have such feelings; but this is a "modern" woman: she initiates sexual activity and when rebuffed by her busy husband "goes for it" elsewhere.

At the time Boas received this story he knew of no other versions of it (1916:739). But Marius Barbeau recorded a version from Mrs Cox in Hazelton in the 1920s and William Beynon got one from Mark Luther in Port Simpson in 1947 (Cove and MacDonald 1987:56, 58-60; also Barbeau 1953:405-08). Each of these versions is different. For Mrs Cox, the "divorce" comes after physical battery; Mark Luther has the husband and wife become beavers together, happily. Thus we see the same "mytheme" in variant forms which reflect the outlook of the story-teller. Tate leans to the magnanimous gesture; for instance, when the wife tells her brothers to "keep my poor husband don't hurt him." And notice the pathos of the brothers' third visit, when the sister/beaver can no longer speak when they ask to take her home, but dives in front of them: "it seems to said that it could do it." This silent plea moves the brothers to drastic action, and her recognition of regret deepens the tragedy.

The story of the hunter's wife change in Beaver

In the olden people among the Natives are very cunnings of hunting, because they are very useful to them animals' skins and their fleshes as the people clothing the animals' skins and also their furs. So they hunts, Grizzly Bears, Black Bear, Mountain Goats they are very useful animals they took wool and spinned wools, and they made it out into yarns after they skins and they woven into dancing blankets or woven into cloaks and many things they are used the wools, and all kinds of animals great and small they have used their skins and almost they have their fleshes as their meat. Therefore their very handed to hunts. So with these family.

   A man was set out

        to hunts for coons

            with his dear wife.

They went to his hunting ground, they been in that place many time before, he has builded his hunting hut there aforetime. Many days are passed by they reached that place, and on the next morning a man went out to put up his traps for coons

            his wife stay

   home

to the camp.

It was late in the
evening a man come home. Two days after he went to see his
traps that he put up a few days ago, he builds many all along in
the valley, when he founds his traps they all have a good catches
and he renewed. He bore his coons to his camp, his wife are very
glad to see her husband good success and

it was late in the night,
he has done all his work. Next morning they stard to skinned their
coons his wife helped him. They dried the skins and also the meats
they both work all day till late in the night. On the next day he
went again to his traps he catches more than he had before. Now
his wife help him to bore them to their camp on the next day early
they begin to skinned their slains the woman are very much happy
for her husband catches many coons,

and the sun shines   to their camp.

She came to where her husband's working. Then she said, My
dear loving husband, just look at my body me for a while. The
man has no time to look at her. He heedless to what his wife said
at first. But she force him to look at her. Then while she compelled
to see her that the man said to her, Your are not better than the
body of these coons.[1] The woman was very much ashame. She
went away weeping from her husband

she seated at the side

of a
little stream

that run between those two mountains

she weeping

there.
But the man care not much about her because he has much work
to do, to his slains. The woman still crying there. Now the man
saw her continued crying he went to her and said to her stop my
dear stop crying come home with me. But she says no I won't, I
am not better than the coon's body I am very much ashame for
what you've said, go away I am not better than the coon's. Then
she commence to crying

So the man went away from her

and go
to his work again.

She keep weeping and ere the sun goes down she felt her body are warm so she ceased her crying she went down to the little stream to cool herself then she took the gravels and small stones
to embankment the water
to make a little deep
and to
swim in it.
Soon the water raise below her knees then she took more stones and also gravels to dam the water, she saw a rock in the centre of the water, she dammed she went and rest on it. Now while the sun goes down
that her husband
went down and call her ashore but she refused him and said I am not better than your coons I am very much ashame for what you've said to me. Then the man saw her swimming around her pond, and late in the night that this man went home, his wife was still in the water all through the night
the man did not sleep he always
heard his wife strike her apron
on the water
in every turn,
early on the next morning he got up and he went down to see his wife he beheld a Lake below their camp and his wife swimming all around it.

Therefore the man stood ashore and he crying come home my dear wife, you know I love you than any one, come home now. Oh come home. Then she said, but you love the coon's body than mine, I will never go back to you again
she still working her
damming,
she always stroke her small leather apron on the water when or before she dive. Then the man was very, very sorry.

In the olden time a women as much as man, the man wear a small piece of leather as an apron between his legs, so it with the women. They use the soft good leather wide as the palm of a hand, they fasten both ends in the belt fasten front and fasten back, and the body was bare, just only loose garment no coats for man no shirts or pants or suits. The woman also has no dress as they do now. So with this woman.

The man keeping watched her several days crying around the Lake calling his wife ashore, her only answered is I am very much ashame for what you've said

      go right down home

                and tell my brothers

                                that I am not die

I shall live in this Lake all alone.

Therefore the man went down to his village. When he reached home, he went to his brothers-in-law and told them his story what became to his wife. Then these six brothers went with their brother-in-law to their hunting ground. When they reached there, behold they see a large Lake between those two mountains and a beaver house in the centre. Then these six brothers stood ashore sorrowfull and their brother-in-law. Now the elder said now my only sister. We are come up to bring you down to our home. Then she swimmed at their front and said, No, I won't, let me, alone, I am alright with my good circumstance. My husband is not angry with me. But I am ashame with my own self. No I will never go down with yours but you can keep my poor husband don't hurt him I will still here all alone. Any time you wanted to come and you shall visit me.

After she said these

    then she dive,

        then those six brothers   lift up their voices   and weeped.

She come out on the water on one side of a large Lake. These brothers went home, sorrow. After two months passed on they went up to that valley again. While they reached there a very great Lake was between those two mountains it was covered all over the valley. They saw their sister diving all around and also they saw three large round things floating in the middle of a large Lake with three Beaver children. (That woman was very good looking woman her hair was brown.)

Now these brothers stood ashore weeping, and their sister came toward them. Then the elder brother said again will you come down with us?

    but she cannot

                speak a word

                       she just dive

                                at the front of them,

her leather apron became a flat beaver-tail and her body was covered with dark brown furs. She was afraid to see her brothers her children swimming around with her, all along. Then her brothers went home again sorry.

These six brother is

can't forget her

ever since.

On the next spring they went again to visit her. They found that large Lake are full with Beavers they stood ashore weeping. As they stood there weeping behold a large Beaver coming toward them with a green cotton tree in her mouth, and

her face was not

yet cover with furs.

Then her elder brother

said to her my only sister will you come down with us? to our home? then she cannot speak just diving at the front of them

it seems to said   that it could do it.

Then these brothers are weep bittery. And they went home once more. Now these brothers are considerate what they can do with their sister, finally they decide to break the dam. So on the next spring they set forth, and went to the Lake that their sister has build. Now they work on to break down the dam. (Before they do their work they saw that large Lake are full with Beavers their sister are not with them.) Then they work on and on till the dam was begin to fell down and the water bursted out and before the dam was empty that numerous Beavers forth from the empty Lake. Then all the Beavers are escape and flee away from them, and scattered all over the Land. But the mother Beavers are not with them. Therefore when the big Lake was empty that these brothers went into the empty Lake to see if their sister will remain there.

They went in

to Beaver's house from houses

at last they

found her

right in the bottom

of the Lake. Her body

are covered

with furs

and her nature face

are still the same

but she cannot

speak,

her claws of her fingers

as animals

and her leather apron is

became

Beaver flat tail

and has their brothers glad

to have her

then

she died right there,

for she had

a dried ground.

Therefore the Natives says that all the Beavers are females, no males at all, because the woman was their Founders, and also the woman's hairs was dark brown so all the Beavers are dark brown furs there is no black furs of Beavers in any one. This is the end.

Note

1 "The body of these coons": There seems to be no specific trait attributed to raccoons by the Tsimshian that would make the hunter's remark particularly insulting. Is Tate implying that she proffered herself to divert the husband from an obsession with the raccoon? She says later: "you love the coon's body [better] than mine."

The Girl Who Married the Bear

The above title is taken from the definitive study of this myth by Catherine McClellan, who calls it "A Masterpiece of Indian Oral Tradition" (McClellan 1970:title page). She is referring to the collective tellings of this popular tale, of which she provides eleven well-documented versions in her monograph. "This was one of the first tales I heard when I began my initial field-work in 1948," she writes (1970:1), "and I was thrilled by the experience."

> Although at that time I knew little of the story's cultural context, I still could sense the tremendous psychological and social conflicts within the plot. For the first time I began to realise that many of the Indian myths that I had been reading in professional collections were more than rather one-dimensional "fairy stories." Today I believe that this particular story attracts the Southern Yukon natives with the same power as does a first-rate psychological drama or novel in our own culture...The story has a good plot with considerable action and suspense, but what probably grips the story-teller and the audience most strongly is the dreadful choice of loyalties that the characters have to make, as well as the pervasive underscoring of the delicate and awful balance between animals and humans, which has existed since the world began (McClellan 1970:1-2).

In some of these tellings the girl and the bear have a real fondness for each other, which leads to the pull of loyalties that Catherine McClellan is referring to. In terms of this kind of dramatic impact, Tate's telling is probably only halfway up the scale of excellence; but we definitely get a sense of it in the scene where the girl-wife asks for a den too difficult for her brothers to find, and then the Bear Chief asks ominously: "How many mats are thy elder brother?"

The history of Kbi'shount

Now in the olden day, there was a very happy people in one of the village of Gitzumkaloun.[1] They live in a very good three row land up the Gitzumkaloun River. I say "three row land"—they was build their village in that three row land. They build their houses at the top of a hill, also they built at the second row under the first, also they built at thirth row under the second row. It's by the side of the river a very good river and the village is not very far from the very large Lake, that they often went there for in the summer for picking wild berries of any kinds all along sides of that large Lake. Hunting ground there also. Those people live there sometimes in the summer for drying wild berries for the winter used. And in winter the hunter use to live there. Therefore they built their little huts on the sides of the large Lake. Many family are builds several huts for their own used in their season.

And there was a great chief in these village
   who had a children four boys and one girl,
      which they love her much.

In those days, that the people of one tribe have their customs to went in one or two days for to catch salmon and let them given to their chief to dry them for the chief use it in winter, or the people went often in their chief's house in winter and the chiefess have them ate some food. So their people work for their chief salmon, also the women, to the chiefess. They went some days and pick berries to their chief's wife. There is no chief and his wife's worked on their own living. Their people work for their living. Also the chief has many slaves male and female slaves, also he has many wifes. Some chiefs has twenty, some ten, and some four wifes. So these slaves and wifes work with the people, but the head wife no work with the people, but the head wife no work as others.

Now those four sons of the chief
    was very cunning of their hunt
        all of them
           was very handy.

The young one has two large beautiful handy dogs. For the animals they are very usefull dogs. One dog's name was "Red" the other was "spots," and these two dogs are very lover of the young girl. This girl's name was
                "Half-summer"
and she very dear to her four brothers, for she's only girl among them.

Now then one day
    the women of the Village
        stard for picking berries
           for their chiefess
Also the young Princess   wanted to go with them.
So they went
    from their camp
        along side
           the large Lake.

Now when they got the berries ground they soon filled their bags with berries. Then the young Princess' bag is not full yet. Soon she slipped on the excrement of Black-bear, which she was wroth she said Oh this big excrement was stick in my foot, alas it very nasty.[2] Thus the Princess said. Then all her companion gather to her, and they fill her basket with berries her basket is not so big as others. Now they stard home to their camp. As they went on that the Princess' line-basket was broken. Then all her berries was scatters on the earth. Her companion come and fill her basket again. They went on again she broke her line-basket now some of them women went away home from her from her, her berries was scatters on ground, mixt with dirt, her few companion gather her berries. They went on. She broke her line-basket again that her companion have said to her let them alone, we have many bags full of berries for you, you don't need for yourselve let's go entate those your berries, let go right on before night lest the wild beasts come and devour us and we will perish, and the young Princess was answered no. I won't leave my berries. Go right on if you wanted.

Now when all them women left her in the woods she was alone there while she gather berries.

Behold
    two young men
        came to her
            which asked her
                what's the matter.
She told them her line-basket was broke several times. They ask her where is her companion. She can't wait her any longer. Therefore these two men ask her to carry her basket to help her, so she consented.

They took her basket full with berries, they went on till they arrived to a Village that she not known to her, she stood out side the large house. Then the father of those young men ask them she not come on with you my son? said he. They said, she stood out-side. Fetch her in. So some two girls went out to take her in, she went in, she sit at one side of the fire.

Soon she sit there
    behold Mouse Woman to her side
        which ask her, don't you know
            who took you here?
The Princess answered, no. The Black-Bear, for you was wroth while you slipped on the excrements while your picking berries, so they took you here. Now took great care. They will give you something to eat, but

don't eat the first salmon.
It is the belly of
the death man.

Now those myth people took the good dry salmon and they roast
it and put it in a dish and lay it at before the Princess but she did
not eat it. They take it back to themselves and ate it. They took the
true salmon and roast it to which Mouse Woman told her it was a
true salmon, so she ate it, also the berries mixt with crab-apples.
But Mouse Woman refuse it, don't taste it. It is the rotten of death
man and the crab-apples are the eyes of the death man, and the
second berries mixt with crab-apples, Mouse Woman say now
that's the good to you, so she ate it, and so on.

Then she became a wife to one of the Black-Bear chief son. She
been there a long while, untill the fall. Every morning the male
Bears went for salmon in the creeks, and the female Bear went in
the woods for picking berries, and in the evening they all come
home.

*Some male Bear are not come home with the rest, and some one
said, My companion salmon line are broken. So the very old bear
have said oh perhaps he use the common bushes, so it broken, cran-
berrie tree are the best for the salmon-lines. Then after two or three
days has been away, he come home with meek. It's because some
person kill some Black-Bear in the creeks, and some female Black-
Bear does the same while the rest come home in the evening, some
one have to said my companion bag-line was broke. She been away
for several days in the woods. Then she come home with slowly.*

Now it was late in the Fall, before the animals go to their Den,
that the Black-Bear chief invites all his tribe, and when all his people are in, he the chief began to ask each family of his people. He
said, What Den will thou lie down this winter? Then one male
Black-Bear answered we shall lie in the Den of so-an-so, they
mention which place they knew to where the Den was, and when
he has through to ask of each family for their Dens, then he turn to
his elder son which married to Kbi'shount (the Princess). The
Black-Bear Chief said I will ask my daughter-in-law, and my elder
son shall answered to me, What Den you need to lie this Winter?
So his son have answered we will lie in the Den of mountain-
beautifull. Then the young Princess have said Oh it is very easy
Den to my younger brother's dog, Red and Spots. So her husband

ask, what do you say at the Den of the side mountain? It's easy to the dog Red and Spots. Then he mention all the Dens he knew to every places, and the woman says it's very easy to her younger brother's dogs Red and Spots. Therefore the Chief says again to his daughter-in-law, Did you wanted a difficulty Den, both side mountains slidding or both side Drum Den? So the young Princess consented she says that place I wanted difficulty Den. Therefore her father-in-law ask her, How many brothers have you my daughter? Soon she answered quickly I have four brothers, she said. The Chief, are they hunters? Princess, yes, they was, all of them are very handy for hunts, so I did not like to have an easy Den to lie this Winter with my husband, lest they could kill us easy. The Chief, Now I'll ask just only one question, is this, How many mats are thy elder brother? Princess, my elder brother's mats are sixty.

Then sixty Black-Bears
> bow their heads
>> and the waters ran down
on each noses.

The sixty mats means sixty times twenty days. That is twenty days lied down by himself alone, and he use one ceder bark mats, and he bath in two days at ten bath in each days.[3] Soon after each bath he went to his wife or if he has no wife he will go to any woman he please and lied down with her. Soon after two days bath and lied with the woman, he took away the mat, and put it aside and took the new mat for the other twenty days. They use this custom when they wanted to succeed the animals. So the Chief Black-Bear ask the young Princess how many mats her elder brother, and those sixty Black-Bears bow their heads they knows that they soon slain by an elder brother of the Princess, so they bow their heads and they crying.

The Black-Bear Chief ask her further on, How many mats are to thy second brother? Princess, my second brother's mats was forty. Then forty Black-Bears bows down their heads the waters rans down on their noses. Again the Chief, How many mats are to thy thirth brother? Princess, My thirth brother's mats are twenty. Then twenty Bears' heads was down with the waters rans down on their noses. The Chief again ask, how many mats are to thy younger brother? Princess, My younger brother's mats are but five. Then five

Black-Bears' heads was down with the water rans down on their nose.

And the husband of the Princess
 also bow down his head
  and the water rans down on his nose.
And at the end of Chief's question then he said to all his myth people, Tomorrow you shall go round all the country and gather much wild carrots for you own use in you Den for Winter. Then the old Bears said we shall lie underneath the olden falling tree. The Chief said to his people soon as you heard the thunder rolling, then at once you shall went to your own Den lest danger shall come upon you.

Next morning all the myth people went round.
 Now soon was the thunder rolling
  each family of Black-Bear went to their own Den.
Now the days of elder brother was fulfill.
 He went for his winter hunting
  His been away for a month among the mountains
   and succeeded sixty Black-Bears
    then he went home.
Another brother that second, his days was fulfill, he went and he been away from home, and he was among mountains a month, he come home. He succeeded forty Black-Bears. Another brother, the thirth, his days was fulfill. He went from home and he has been among the mountains a month. Then he went home. He succeeded twenty Black-Bears. Then he come home.

Now the younger brother days was fulfill. He went with his two dogs that is Red and Spots. Now he went on and on he did not gain any thing, and he went farther on, many days has passed and did not gain any thing, so he stood at foot one of the mountain crying thinking his sister that was loset last summer.

Now while he was crying
 his two dogs lift up their noses
  they went up to a both side slidding mountain
   soon their reached up to where the few trees was.
 The young man hear the dogs barking up there.
  Then the young man

cease his crying, looking up to where his two dogs are barking. He saw his two dogs raning around barkings and see his dogs sometimes they wave their tails. Therefore the young man try to climb up to the mountain side, wear on his snow-shoes *that hunters, when they climb the mountain they out the ends or the points of mountain goats' horns in the bottoms of snow-shoes it's four horns' points on each side.* So this young man were trying reach to where his dogs are barking and he had his long cane. *The hunters' cane are long one seven or eight foot long and they put the horn on one end. When went on the slidding snow they use this cane, so it won't slipp.* Now he went and it's very hard to went up quickly, for the snow is too slippe. Then his dogs still barking, but the young man cannot go up any further. He always slidding back for the snow is too soft. Alas he stood there and not half way from the foot of the slidding snow his face towards where his dogs are barked.

Now he was thinking that he won't got up there.

Then he wanted to turn back.

His sister look down at him, she put forther her hand

and she took some snow and she pressed

Then she roll it down.

Then young man see the little rolling snow come down and struck the front end of his snow-shoe.

Then the young man
took it up
and look at it. Behold
the four fingers of some person
pressed around the snow.

Now the man try again to climb up finally he reached up his dogs still barked, and put their ears down and waved their tail. He come at mouth of a Den. Now when the dogs reached to where the young woman was, that the Princess knew her brother's dogs, Red and Spots. For the Princess called them by their names Red and Spots so those dogs wave their tails and down their ears for they knew her also, yet dogs see the Black-Bear seated with her, so they barked. Now the man went, he see his sister was in the Bear Den.

Then the Princess call him to her,
    and she said wait my brother
        untill I give birth.
She born two children, she hand them to her brother that stood out side the Den. So he took them and put them in side his hunter garment. Now the Princess forth from the Den.
    She has said to her brother,
        now my dear don't kill thy brother-in-law
            with knife or spear or arrow,
                just make a smoke in his Den.
Then the young man has said to his sister,
    I will not kill him.
        But Princess said, no, not so my brother,
kill him, but don't use the spear,
    if you kill him not
        then you shall die.
Therefore the young man made fire at the mouth of his brother-in-law's Den, and the smoke was full in the Den. Soon they heard his brother-in-law groaned in his Den, and soon they heard the groaned was ceased. Then he put out the smoke he knew that he was died.

        The young man went in and draw him out, and while he lied at the mouth of his Den, the Princess have a sang. At the end of her singing she said to her brother, now dear cut him. The man just put his knife at Bear's breast, she sang again, with moarned. *It's before young man reached the place to where the Den was, that Black-Bear teached his Princess how to sing as soon as he die, and when he cut, it will sing again, and when they dried his skin the other song and at roast the Bear's heart another song, and when the skin was dried then put the red-ore at back from head to tail, and put also red-ore across under arms. Thus the Bear have said to his wife the Princess, and they shall put my skin at the side of a fire to dried it. When you hear a little crake noise, then you shall know that I am chilly and you shall make more fire. Thus said the Bear to her.*[4]

Now after the young man cut the Bear, he rolled down the Bear. Then they both slidding down on the snow, with his sister and two cubs. They went right home. This young man was very glad to succeed his loving sister. And when they arrived at their home, then the people of the three row Village are gather together they see the Princess and her two cubs. Soon those people see her come home again make joyful noise for gladness. Her father make a great feasting and give his grantchildren names.

And the children soon grow they both boys. Every morning they played out, and inside, and when they saw little clouds arose among the hills, they said
>   There is
>   see my myth people grantfather smoke.
Therefore the hunters went and kill Bears,
>   and many times they
>   saw the smokes.[5]
>   So on the next day
>   they played inside
>   their grantfather's house
>   ran around
knocked down each other, and ran around behind the people that was sitting around the fire. Grantfather love them most. On the next day again they arose from their bed. They ran around in the house, knocking each other.

Now while they played
>   that the other fell down
>   against their grantmother's back
>   that the old woman fell back fainted.
And the whole people in the house raise and worked to the old woman to relieve her faint, and she revived again she was distressed, she groaned and she said, Oh those little slaves that hurt me, we don't know where come from.

These children were much ashame to what their grantmother have said to them. They wept bittery also their mother was ashame. She wept also. Then these children went to their mother, and they ask her to their leave the Village, and they want to go among their father's myth people. Their mother said to them don't come back any more, you might stay with your father, among his myth people, and bring food to me sometimes, and give animals to younger uncle. So they went on their way, sorrowful mother was very sorrow. Now Grantfather mist them.   *That the end.*

Notes

1 "Gitzumkaloun": Kitsumkalum, a village at the mouth of the Kitsumkalum River, a tributary of the Skeena, near the present-day Terrace, B.C. Other storytellers Place the events of the legend in other locales (Boas 1916:836).

2 "Very nasty": Tate's heroine is rather genteel in her reproach. Compare, for instance, Minnie Johnson in de Laguna's careful transcription (1972:880-81):

> "Big flappy foot, always pooping in a place where you
> can step on it!"

and again:

> "Big flapper foot, never get out of the way to do his job,
> right on the road!"

3 "Ten bath in each days": This has caused some confusion. Boas interpreted it as taking a bath every other day (1916:449). But if the hunter is supposed to lie alone for twenty days then there can be no bath followed by woman during that period. What seems to be meant here is a twenty-day abstinence from bathing and sex, followed by two days of abundance, i.e. ten times a day, to make up for the twenty missed days. Then you get a new mat.

4 "The Bear to her": Instructions for the ritual treatment of the bear carcass are an essential element of this story. Tate forgot this, and had to add the Bear's final words out of sequence. Maria Johns gave Catherine McClellan the following rendition of the dialogue prior to the parting of the girl and the Bear:

> "You're my wife, and I am going to leave soon. It looks like your brothers are going to come up here soon, before the snow is gone. I want you to know that I am going to do something bad. I am going to fight back!"
>
> "Don't do it!" she said. "They are my brothers. If you really love me, you'll love them too. Don't kill them. Let them kill you! If you really love me, don't fight! You have treated me good. Why did you live with me, if you are going to kill them?"
>
> "Well, all right," he said, "I won't fight, but I want you to know what will happen." His canines looked like swords to her. "These are what I fight with," he said. They looked like knives to her. She kept pleading.
>
> "Don't do anything. I'll still have my children if they kill you!" She knew he was a bear then. She really knew

They went to sleep. She woke again. He was singing again.

"It's true," he said. "They are coming close. If they do kill me, I want them to give you my skull—my head, and my tail. Tell them to give them to you. Wherever they kill me, build a big fire, and burn my head and tail and sing this song while the head is burning. Sing it until they are all burnt up!" [Maria sang the song again...] (McClellan 1970:31)

5 "Saw the smokes": Jake Jackson's version (McClellan 1970:20) has the sister helping the younger brother to spot the bears' dens. It is explained that "the bear lives just like a person. He has a fire, and it smokes right in his den." The sister looks up into the hills and sees the smoke. "She can tell how many bears there are too. Just the woman can see the smoke. Nobody else can" (McClellan 1970:20). In Tate's story it is the innocent cubs whose extra-sensory perception aids the hunters against their father's "tribe."

FABLES

Porcupine and Grizzly Bear

We always welcome a tale in which a bully gets his comeuppance. The Grizzly Bear is acting true to form here. He knows what everybody knows—that Porcupine can induce frosty weather and clear up the annoying rain; but he is so stupid in his brutality that he cannot even recognize when he is getting his own way, and keeps on with his violence. In the end he gets his frost.

Melville Jacobs has tried to analyze in psychological terms the Grizzly's "psychotic personality" and the "sado-masochistic partnership" which he sees exhibited in some stories (Jacobs 1959:63). We suspect that it is an important element in this vignette that the victimized porcupine is female rather than male, reflecting a cultural attitude, perhaps a universal attitude, of the not-so-distant past. Whether or not Jacobs has enough evidence to justify the psychological interpretations he offers, his comment on prevailing social mores in the tribes known to him seems eminently applicable to the story before us: "A woman's policy, again, was not so much to be passive as to be judicious, overtly unaggressive, and to survive. She must be realistic, bide her time, and await favorable opportunity to hit back" (Jacobs 1959:170).

The History of Porcupine

While the time in the Fall
  when all the animals went into their Dens,
    also the great Grizzly Bear sat into his own Den
      for Winter sleep,
and the great rain descended
  and therefore the drops of water in the great Grizzly Bear's den,
    and his fur is full of water
      and he was disappoint as long as the rain.
So he sat at the door of his Den   looking out for some thing.

And while he was there,   Behold a Porcupine coming along.
As she passed the door of
  great Grizzly Bear Den,
    that Grizzly Bear said,
      will you come in here my friend,
        I will sup with you.
Therefore the Porcupine turn   in the great Grizzly Bear's Den.

Then the Grizzly Bear make a large fire. Then he caught the poor Porcupine, and bind her foot and hands and put her near the fire and burnt her back fur with fire. Then the great Grizzly Bear have said to Porcupine, while he was burnt her back fur, Make frost, you little unsightly animal. Du'du'uh says the great Grizzly Bear. Yes, I will do[1] said the Porcupine. Master, loose my binds, then I will do what you want.

But the great Grizzly Bear

won't hear her

what the poor

Porcupine said to him.

Because he was great and strong he has power over all animals so he did not hear what poor animal that is the Porcupine have said to him. His prout heart was against her. Then he kick her into the fire once more.

Make frost,
you little ugly Porcupine,
du'du'uh,

said the great Grizzly Bear. He mocked the poor Porcupine. Then the back fur of Porcupine burnt.   *So all the porcupine back not much fur now.*

Now when these poor weak animal almost dead
    for she scorched her skin
        she said to great Grizzly Bear,
have mercy on me sir   I will do for what you wanted.

Then again the Grizzly Bear kicked her against the fire, said the same words, Make a frost, you little unsightly animal. The great Grizzly Bear done it many times, and when the poor thing was dying, he thrown her out side his Den. There she layed a long while, and when she opened her eyes, and tried to walk away, with pain all over her body, she began to say, You big ugly great power Grizzly Bear, don't say anything if you frozen to dead in your Den. Then she walk away slowly, and she began to sing a song her moarning song,

As I was walk at the foot of a beautiful green leaved mountain[2]
    Then all the stars of heaven are glittering as the sky's all
            clear for North wind.

She repeated this four times

                        with crying

                                    at the end of four
times.

Then the North wind began to blew and all the stars of the sky was twinkles as the North wind signs to blew hart. Then the North wind blew hart and it became very cold and every thing was frozen. Now the great Grizzly Bear was also frozen to dead in his Den.

For he was mock

                   with weak and smaller

                              than himself.

The great Grizzly Bear thought to himself while he was mocking to the weak and little poor Porcupine, that no one could take the poor Porcupine out from his hand. But the North wind avenge the poor weak animal, for her foes.

Notes

1 "I will do": Could Tate be punning on "du'du'uh," the apparently untranslatable Tsimshian expletive? In any case, it is no problem for Porcupine to make frost. Stith Thompson cites all the widespread stories of Porcupine trapped on Beaver's island and making a frozen pathway in order to escape to the opposite shore (Thompson 1929:302). Tate sent to Boas his own version of this "Porcupine and Beaver" tale in tandem with the present story (Boas 1912:227; notes in Boas 1916:724-27).

2 "Green leaved mountain": one remembers the chiefly name of Porcupine, "Sea-otter of Green Side Mountain," in the previous story (above). The porcupine mainly feeds on the tender inner bark of conifers. The song is a meteorological incantation effective in hypnotizing the weather.

Grizzly Bear and Beaver

Tate obviously did not like bullies. The closed societies of the coast must have bred their share of grizzlies in human form. What could a sensitive youth—as Tate undoubtedly was—do against the inherent totalitarian authority of the chiefs but dive down deep into himself and watch them become bogged down by their boastfulness?

This story is truly of the Aesop's fable type, where the animals represent human traits. It has no comment to make on hunting practices or other tribal customs, only on the universal condition of the human heart.

The story Grizzly Bear and Beaver

Many years ago there was a great Lake was at the side of the Skeena River where many beavers build their house because a deep water there and a safely hiding place and a very good sheltering for them in the winter time many olden houses of beaver and many new houses as well and they thought that the dangers enemy was away from them

and

on

the

next

day

those beavers
thoughtless that there was no danger near them. Therefore they leave their house and went out for fresh air so covers all over the melting ice in the early spring while sleeping animals was wake and walk out from their Dens.

A Grizzly Bear just out from his winter sleeping as soon as he went out he beheld a many beavers was covers all over the ices. He went there secretly and he fall on them and slew many of them. And some of them was escape from him to their houses in the Lake, and the great Grizzly Bear hunt them to their house and he slew many of them in their houses,

and they griefs.

The great Grizzly Bear was happy because he has much food and those poor weak beavers was great griefs.
He thought the flesh of all those beavers are enough for him through the summer food.

Only one beaver was escape from his paws.

The poor Beaver went down way in the deep water, and the great Grizzly Bear ate all his flesh. When he was satisfy he lay down there and sleep around his slains. And a poor lonely Beaver hide in the deep.

And she thought of the great enemy and she think if she can made a false ground at one side of a large Lake so she took all the wet soft moss and she gather at the close of a fallen tree that stretched at the side of a large Lake. She build there in the night, for she was afraid to work in the day time. She made like a dry land and old fallen tree was on the dry land that the Beaver has build.

And when the summer is ended when the salmon were on the creeks, now the great Grizzly Bear's flesh beavers now are all gone that the Great thing was very hungry. He was walking around the Lake to searched his prey. He went to the creeks and catches many salmons in the creeks to be food in the winter. And on the next day, as he went around in his very hungry, as he proudly walking stronger than any beasts, he stood there and behold a poor weak Beaver was sitting at the end of a fallen tree yonder a lowly sitting there. While the proud Beast see her sitting there he ask her with his proud voice, what you been doing there you poor lowly animal? says the proud Grizzly Bear. As he look her sitting at the end of an old log

The Grizzly Bear shall die.

Then Grizzly Bear ask her, what? says he. Again the Beaver said once more,

The Grizzly shall die.

Then the great Grizzly Bear was angry. Who that shall die you have said? But she not care to answer him. He walk down to and fro on the dry land at the root of a fallen tree, where the poor Beaver sitting at the end of it. Again the Beaver said once more,

The great Grizzly Bear shall die.

Yes, says the great Monster animal, I will kill you right there don't run away I will tear your flesh right now

and he   walk

toward   the Beaver

that seated there. With his proud heart he has walking on the log. Don't go away I will devour your flesh. Again the brave Beaver said,

The Great Grizzly shall die.

And the proud heart Grizzly ran in rage, but the poor Beaver sit there, had little swimmed out there she look back at the Grizzly Bear.

The Grizzly Bear shall die.

Then the Great Grizzly Bear jump on the Beaver. Therefore the Beaver was dive under the fallen tree right in the false ground that the Beaver was build to entrap the great Grizzly Bear

And the great Monster

was struggle in the slough

that the Beaver has build.

Then the Beaver come out on the surface. She went on the log the same place as she sat before. She look at the great Grizzly Bear was struggling there. She said once more, The Grizzly Bear shall die. So the Grizzly Bear was tire in the mud there and he groan in despair. He use all his might to try to get away from the slough. But he would not because the soft mud keep him he try to swim but he can't and before he die there he said to the Beaver

Come and help me.

But the Beaver said again, The Grizzly Bear shall.

Now the great animal to howling and crying

which rent through

the woods, and moaned

and he died there

with great despair

and he drowned in the slough.

Because he was not pity to those weak animals he tried to devour all the weak animals. He thought that no one beside himself. Yet the weak one stronger than him in wisdom. Only one weak animal kill him he howling and crying. While he slayers all the poor beavers, no beavers crying or moaned when the Mighty Grizzly Bear destroyed them.

Therefore let not the stronger oppressed the poor or weak, for the weak shall have the victory over the Mighty. This is the end.

COSMOLOGY

Sun, Moon, and Fog

Boas did not ask for a story of this kind. Tate volunteered a Tsimshian cosmology. His title, which mentions only sun and moon, seems to indicate he set out to tell just the myth of the brothers, as he remembered it (remembering it quite differently from any known analogue, as it happens); but an urge to be comprehensive in writing what amounts to an encyclopedia entry leads him to interpolate material on the length of months and their names. Other small details add to the impression that Tate has improvised the sort of "school lesson" that was given to children.

One is tempted to see this, in its present form, as an original bit of creative writing on Tate's part. The pitch-hoop mask for the sun-brother is not found elsewhere that we have record of. His having to hasten across the sky, with his sister wrestling him to a stop at midday, these are vivid and apparently original images. The little slave trying to get the people excited about the new moon rising is also a memorable image, unique in its dramatic (and obviously Biblical) diction, as is the picture of the sister shaking out her wet garments at the fire and causing all the fog in the world. In suggesting that this may be the first manuscript penned by a British Columbia creative writer we can only be tentative; for it is indeed possible that this narrative is exactly as told by old people whom Tate consulted. It doesn't feel like it though.

The History of sun and moon

It was about in the early days of before the Creation.

There was no human being was livining on earth or any other places, but the lord in heaven was live there.

And there was no light in heaven at that time but heaven was with[1] form and void, and darkness was in heaven.

And the Lord of heaven has two sons and one daughter, and many myth people them quadruped animals, and this Chief call them his people.

These are the names of his three children.

First boy's name, "Early-Morning-Traveller-Round-The-Sky" and the second son name was Shazapanilth or "Journey-From-The-Easther-to-Westher," and the girl's name was "Steadying-The-Sun."

The second boy is so very sound and bravest and so cleverest than his elder brother.

So the next day tbe second boy (Shazapanilth) make off his mind, and thinking about the deep darkness that covered them often, so the next day he (Shazapanilth) said to his sister let's go and carry down pitchy wood.

And so they went and have a best smears wood in much, and make a hoop out one of the ceder tender branch.

And he measure around his face, and fasten the smears wood around the hoop, and he put it on his face like a mask.

And when he has done it, then he said to his sister that was with him when he was carried the pitchy wood with him, See that no man should know this.

And so he went toward the Eastern skys and he appear from there to the myth people.

He (Shazapanilth) burnt them pitchy wood around the hoop on his face with fire.

And as soon as these myth people saw the shining light from the Eastern skys, they all feel happy to see the shining light.

Then he (Shazapanilth) run fast as he could, from the East to West with the mask of fire on his face.

He run fast lest his smears wood should consume, so he run quickly through the skies.

And all the myth people gather together around their Master and have a council.

And they said we are so great pleased to see thy son give us light to lighten us, but he was too faster through the skys so we won have little longer, let him run little slow then we have little longer light.

And the Chief invite his son Shazapanilth, and told him what the myth people said.

And (Chief) his son says that he can't help it lest his smears wood mask will consume before he reach to the West.

And again he went on every days.

And again them myth people have council once more and their request to let their prince slowly traveller through the sky.

And soon the maid said ("Steadying-The-Sun") I wrestle him when he traveller through the skys.

And all the myth people thank her, and also father thank his daughter.

And it was so that Shazapanilth went out towards the Eastern skies, and the maid out also towards the south-western skies, and soon her brother arise up in the Eastern skys and she ("Steadying-The-Sun") run back to met her brother.

And she said Just wait me till I met you. Just wait till I met you.

And she run with all her might till she wrestled him right in the middle of the skies.

And the sun still in the midst of heaven, little longer, and the maid stand firm wrestled her brother.

So we see the sun rest a moment[2] *in the midst of heaven, or stayed little longer in midst of heaven.*

And when the myth people saw that the sun stayed little longer in the midst of heaven, they begun to shouting for a great joy, and they said "Steadying-Of-The-Sun" wrestled by the sun.

And all the multitudes of heaven make a great joy.

And soon the Chief of heaven was wroth and scold his elder son for his not cleverest as you youngest brother.

Then elder just bow down his head and cry for his father scolding.

And when his brother (The Sun) came in and lie down for his weary traveller, and "Early-Morning-Traveller" said to his little boy slave, while all the myth people slept and all his father's house was slept also, and after he said thus he rub the charcoal on one side of his face, he said to his little boy slave,

When thou see I am raise up from the East and you must make a joyful noise, then you shall say this hurrah hurrah hurrah for his coming, he is come.

And he went towards the East, and his brother (Sbazapanilth) was a deep sleep for his wearisome, and his shining face beamy out through the smoke stark.

Then his brother "Early-Morning-Traveller" raise up from the East, and the little slave boy make a noise leaping, and said Holla, Holla, He is coming. Hurrah Hurrah, He has coming.

And some of the myth people asked him, you coon what makes you such a noise for?

He (slave) still joyful and leaping and he point toward East, and all the myth look up and saw, behold the Moon raise up from the East, and all the myth people make a great shout Hurrah, Hurrah.

Soon they were came together, they all assemble, all kinds of animals were have a great council.

And they all consent together that the sun will go round every day to keep the world light, warm and make every thing good and better, by the sun.

And they also was very please to the moon.

Then again they have a large council all kinds of different animals were assemble. The dogs there were too. The dogs were wiser animals than all the rest. So they spoke first in the animal's council. Then the wise council spoke and said (dog) let the moon visible into forty days and then shall be invisible. And they all silents not one animals spoke a word. Then those dogs set together on one side talking over the matter and then the wise dog stood still lifting up his fingers to number forty days in each month. And while he has done this that someone strike the wise man's thumb (dog's thumb). And porcupine said while he strike the thumb of dog down and said who will live then when forty days in each month[3] through the year round? So let the thirty days in each month. And then all the different kinds of animals' council well satisfy, and consent, and all animals said let us follow on for what the porcupine has been said. So the month's days now are thirty and there's twelve month in each year, and all animals said agree that they need not the dogs be among them.

So it is that the dogs hates all kinds of beast of the field. And the dogs' first enemy was a porcupine for the porcupine strike dog's thumb with his spining tail while they was in the council. And it's because the porcupine took away dogs' high place among the animals, so the dog hate them porcupines, until now. Then thumb of dogs way back in the middle of his fore paws now. They say there were six toes on each paws of dogs on that time so the number months twelve on that day. And now that the days of porcupine we have thirty days in each months.

And all the myth people have light in the upper world and our earth was still darkness was in the deep. And again the myth people give names to every months through the year round, when they were in council. They commence to number

> the months between October and November, "the month of the Brushwood falls"
> and between November and December, name "Nazarite"[4]
> and between December and January, "months of long days"
> and between January and February, "month of Caught of Spring Salmon"
> and between February and March, "month of Oolachan ate"
> and between March and April, "Boiling month"
> and between April and May, "month seals' cubs"

and between May and June, "month of Eggs"
and between June and July, "month of sockeye salmon"
and between July and August, "month of Humpbacks"
and between August and September, "month of wild berries
    picking"
and between September and October, "month of toys top"[5]
and they have four season through year round, Spring, Summer, and Fall and Winter.

And when the sun (Shazapanilth) was sleep and the sparking forth from his mouth so it make the stars in the night.

And the moon gets her light from the shining face of the sun[6] while he was slept for he wearisome and his sun beamys out through smoke stark.

And sometimes he (Sun) was happy and rub his face with his sister red ochre.

And the people knew what kind weather today or tomorrow.

When the people saw the red sky in the evening, and they knew it shall be fine weather tomorrow.

And if they saw red clouds in morning,[7] and they knew the bad weather shall be today.

Thus said the people now.

And the maid make up her mind so the next day she went toward the west, gather her garment and strike the water.

And she come back home quickly.

And her father the Chief ask his daughter from whence come thou my daughter?

Then the maid said I am come from the west for a journey.

And she stood around her father's large fire to warm herself with her garments on.

Then she shake her garments to let the water off and the water from her garment off to the fire.

And the fogs went out from her father's house, and the fogs covers all over the myth people's Village.

And all the myth people felt refresh themself from the heat of the sun, and they all very pleased to this maid for she give them their refresh.

It is so that the fogs come from West.

And the father of those three princes were happy to see his children wisdom.

And he give his (Chief) blessing to his three children.

He gave to his elder son (Moon) to ruled the whole year round, to let his people understood the season of the year.

And He (Chief) also gave his blessing to his second son (Shazapanilth) to ruled the days, and his second son will brought good things to the whole world, fruitfulness and fatness, by his shine.

And also he gave his blessing to his daughter that she will refresh his people from their wearison with her cool soft fogs.

That end.

Notes

1 "With": Tate obviously intended to write "without form, and void" (Genesis 1:2).

2 "The sun rest a moment": The belief that the sun slows at its zenith is not known to be held generally among the Tsimshian. This mytheme is a variation of the Greek Phaëthon story, brought into North America as the "sun snarer" or the "sun substitute" theme (Thompson 1929:42-45); in the Northwest it is usually Mink who takes over the sun and causes consternation by erratic behavior. Tate differs in proposing the stopping of the sun as a desirable thing, and indeed as an observed fact.

The source of this idea may have been in a naming ritual, the kind of show that was popular in the long winter nights. William Beynon writes the following note to a somewhat similar story from a later informant, Dan Green:

> In 1917 the writer was at Hazelton during a dramatization of the name "Going from one side to the other of the Heavens"...In the singing of the dirge song when the name was announced, then a drum affair containing a gasoline light cleverly concealed in a drum which was transparent and an arc was described across the rear wall of the house and when the portion of the dirge song commanding the sun to stop in its path the drum structure halted in its arc and then the song continued and the drum went over and disappeared to the other side (Columbia MS Beynon 189).

3 "Forty days in each month": Traditionally the debate between the dogs and the porcupines is not over the number of days in a month but over the number of months assigned to winter and summer. Tate may have had in mind to say that a forty-day month would make winter too long, but he doesn't quite get it said.

4 "Nazarite": an unexpected reference to Christmas. The Tsimshian word that Tate uses here is the one usually translated as "taboo"—"taboo month" (Boas 1916:115), November-December being the *halait* season devoted to spiritual training, rituals and dances. It could, in Christian terms, be called the "holy month."

5 "Toys top": Sidney Campbell of Metlakahtla told H.S. Wellcome in 1917 a similar set of names for the months, but he attached the spinning-top to January: "[T]hey wanted to hurry it because it was a dangerous month, and that is the reason they played with the tops [rubbing hands together briskly] to hurry the month" (U.S. National Archives MS). Boas describes top-spinning as taking place on the frozen-over river (1916:409).

6 "Face of the sun": Had Tate learned from European sources the scientific fact of the moon's light being a reflection of the sun's light? Or was it from the same source as his information that the stars come from the sun's snoring mouth?

7 "Red clouds in the morning": shepherd's warning. Yorkshire people have known this saying from time immemorial. Have the Tsimshian known it also?

MORAL TALES

The Blind Husband

A blind husband's revenge on a greedy wife has been told and retold over a wide area of North America (Thompson 1929:354). The wife is secretly planning for a better marriage, but she has stuck by her ailing husband up to this point and brought up a rather well-adjusted male child. Perhaps, no more than with the abandoned boy myth should we take these matrimonial circumstances as indicating actual tribal mores rather than creating an interesting plot. In any case, the story-teller's audience wanted to imagine this predicament—what to do about a useless blind husband, what to do when one's dissatisfied wife is pushed to homicidal thoughts. Then there is the miraculous cure to think about—usually through the agency of the Loon. The blind man had seen too many "bad things." The Loon, as a diving bird, might symbolize a cleansing baptism.

One thing that Tate adds is a full expression of the love of the son for the father, which at the end turns into silence at the pleas of his mother. This is a very touching but disturbing element. The boy drops out of the story, and we wonder about him. The husband does not escape the consequences of his revenge; it follows him everywhere as the hooting of an owl. This is a nervous story.

The story of a poor blind Giatkada

There was a camp of a blind man at the mouth of one creek he use to camp there afore time before he was blind while he was a great hunting. Hiswife is with him and his little son which love him much. They camp there waiting the salmon shall run up the creek they had a little hut a good hunting little. They waiting a long time for salmon, until the fall. Then when the salmon on the creek a woman and their son went up the creek and catch few salmon by they strike with a pole with a dart of bone on the end of it, carried them down their hut where the old blind hunter is. And while the leaves are falling (it's before all the wild beasts are went to their Dens) very early on the next morning the woman said that she will gather barks for winter fire. So they did. She always went with her little son lately in the evening they come home. They done it every day.

Now very early on the next morning a boy went out, while was sitting outside he look over yonder. Behold a great Grizzly Bear coming down by the side of a stream looking for the old dead salmon for to eat before he was long sleep in his Den in the long winter. Therefore the boy ran in and he told to his blind father that a Great Grizzly Bear coming down yonder. Then the blind man says

take me forth

so the boy took him by the hand and lead him outside. Then he said again

ran in and take my Bow and my good arrow.

Then the boy did as his father have said. He brought him bow and one good arrow. Then he give it to his blind father. Now his father said once more

Now take at the end of my arrow and point it at the elbow of that great Grizzly Bear that I might shot his heart.

Therefore the boy did what his father said. He took the point of an arrow, and point the Grizzly Bear's elbow end. Now the boy said

Now shooted it.

Then the old hunter use all his might to pull open his bow and he shot it. The arrow went right through the great Grizzly Bear's heart, and lay there dead. Then the old hunter said I shot him only once! For he heard that Grizzly Bear cried alouder, blind man heard the Grizzly Bear groaning, a short time and ceased. He said again now his dead for I shot right into his heart.

Then his wife come forth and mocked him and she said O yes you shot him to dead. The blind man said

Yes I did shot him.

Then his wife laught at him.

(The woman know that he shot the Bear to dead, yet she not wanted to give the Grizzly Bear meat to him, so she said that her blind husband missed his shooting. For she thought when her husband die soon and she will have married again to a better man than him.)

Now lately in the afternoon that the woman said to his son let us go over yonder my son

for barking
we shall be back late
in the evening.
They went
over to where the great Grizzly Bear lay dead. When she reached
there she said to the boy, Now my son don't
tell
your father
that
he did shot this Grizzly Bear. You and I together shall eat the
meats and tallows of this great Grizzly Bear. Then she cut into
pieces. She filled up her canoe twice, and it was very lately in the
evening she come home
after she washed the arrow thoroughly.
And the blind man ask did you find my arrow dear. The boy says
I yes my father.
Bring it to me.

Then his wife brought to him, and she said here's your arrow
that you shots the old lying tree there. Then the old hunting took
his good and successful arrow and he feeling and smelling and he
said, yes I know that I have shots the beast now
I smelled the fume of tallow.
Then his wife was wrath on him.
He said once more
On this my successful arrow have I smelled
the tallows of Great Grizzly Bear.

Every morning she went for barking with her son. She build a
large fire and cooked as much as she want for the Great Grizzly
Bear meats and tallows. They eat all they want with son it was late
in the evenings every at day she come home and she often advice
her little son that he will not told his father that he did shot the
Great Grizzly Bear lest he ate meats and they soon gone and you
and I shall both die with starvation, so let him die because his too
old and blind, he's no use.
But the young lad
would not listen
what her adviced him daily.
His love was much
to his old father.

He always with him in his old rag bed, and sleep with him often.

One night they went to bed early. Then the lad whisper his old father. Father, says he, you have shooted that great Grizzly Bear last few days ago and here is a little meat which I hide it behind my ear, because my mother not wanted me to tell you that we had plenty lest you ate the meats and tallows. We always eat meats and tallow every day. My mother made a large fire up there, and she cooked many meats and tallows. She said that she will whip me if I told you this.

> Here I give you
>> this little meat
>>> eat my father
>>>> I don't want you to die
>>>>> do eat this father.

But his father refused and said go on my dear son you ate it. Then he, the old man, begun to crying,

>>>>>> and crying the whole night.

And before the day light he said to his son, Now dear son I want you to lead me and guide me on the trail that leads toward the Lake up in the woods yonder. Then the lad asked his father

> what you gone to do pa.

>>>> Then he answered
I will stay there and comfort myselve. And the lad says once, No I won't do it my father lest you die. And the old man said once more

> If you love me
>> my son and you will do what I have said.

>>>> And the boy consented
and said but don't kill youselve. No, no, the old man said, but let not your mother know it.

And they went little further down from their hut. They got into the trail that leads up to the Lake. They went on and on till they arrived at the Lake. And the old man said now go back to your mother my lad, and let me sitting down here. And the lad ask him to stay with him there, but he sent him down to his mother. They both crying, and they are parting.

>>> The boy went down,
and the old man sitting there alone, crying,

>>>> crying a whole day

nothing
            could stop him.

After a while it was near the sun set that he heard a Loon shouting out on the Lake sea. The blind man still crying. Again he hear
the Loon little closer to where he sitting. Then he still weeping.
Then thirth time he heard the Loon right close to him, and little
later on someone touched by his side, which asked him and said,
    Man, why weeps thou?
                    He answered, Oh Genius, genius, I was
in great despair, and my wife had despiteful use me.
    But what you wanted me to do for you? says the good genius.
Then the blind man says
                    good genius that I may receive my sight.
        Then Genius said now turn toward me. The poor blind
man hasten to turn towards the genius. Then the genius take a rub-
bishys from his right eye, and then his left eye. The genius
throwed these mingled mass on the water. He said to the blind
man
        Now did you see me?
    And blind man have said yes. I just show little light.
    So the Genius put his hands and took some more bad blood off
from his eyes, and said
            you are heedless hunter
                why don't hide your face
                    while bad things passed
                        at your front of your sitting?
                    Now tell me
                        if you can see yonder?
    The blind man said is not very clear   sir. Then Genius done it
three times, and when the Genius done it four times he was vanished from his sight. Therefore the blind man went in to the water
behold all kind of rubbish are full in there, blood, ashes, hairs,
smokes, steams, dusts and so on. He was very glad, and he wanted
to know how was opened his eye.

On the next morning he hide himself lest his son come up and
see him. Now very early on the next morning a young lad wake
up and he run up the trail up to the Lake, and when he reached a
place to where his old blind father sitting no one to be found and

he begun to crying and call by his loving father, but no answered. He saw a blood in the water he thought some bad beast ate him in the night so he was very sorry. He went down the trail crying and calling along the way. His mother hear him crying, coming down the trail. She wake up and ran out wanted to know who was there. Behold the lad coming along crying and said some wild beasts had devoured my poor father. The lad mother was angry to her son, and she said stop crying let us happy for your father was dead, come on eat these richly meats, stop stop at once or I'll whip you. There the lad was afraid to her. He cease crying and he not eat much. He was think   over his father.

At the end of their eating she said to the lad, Let us go for barking. The lad lay down on his old father's bed weeping. His mother went alone. She went on the trail, and when she reached the place she saw some thing dragged down into the water, and she saw blood and mingled with rubbish. She believed that her husband died and she was glad.

She went little further down the trail she saw a large pile of thick barks at the distance along side the trail, so she went towards it and pile some more. Now the man went down on the other way. He heard his wife happy song for he died, instead of moarning song. He passed her, and he went right down to the hut. Behold his son lying on his bed, crying.

He said to him

My dear son

I am still alive

and also my eyes open   and I can see clearer.

Don't cry, come on, let us close every holes around this hut, and I shall shuts firm close the door. Let your mother stay out the door tonight. And after their eating their supper they went to bed with his loving son.

Later on in the evening the woman come home and the door was shut against her. She knock the door, and said dear son did your father come home? or you're still alone? But no answered from them, and she says to her husband dear have compassing on me, for I have much cold out here. Still no answered from them, and she feel very cold. Will you open the door for me dear son? and her voice shaken on account of her very cold. She said be pity on me lest I am frozen out here.

And before day light

she transformed
 in Owl
 she hooting.
Then the man ran and open the door. He beheld an Owl flew away from him. She seat on a tree which stood near by their hut and she hooting much. So the man said to her go away you Owl among the woods.
 And he has
 a great hunter again
 once more.

But not many years passed on. He went by himself alone in the mountain. He often heard Owl hooting every night since his wife transform in Owl. On the next night when he was alone in the mountain he also heard the Owl hooting over yonder there and he said, you foolish woman get away from me I did not want you to come near my camp. Then the Owl's hooting was ceased she heard her husband says, and the man forget he was talking to the Owl. He went forth from his booths that the Owl flew above his head and he fell down dead right there.

This is the end.

The Deserted Youth

If one takes this story literally, one has to accept that a chief has so much pride of position in Tsimshian society that he will abandon his son to almost certain death for quite petty misconduct. It should be punishment enough to have the youth bear the brunt of his three uncles' sarcasm. To leave him behind to starve is what a family counsellor would call "over-reacting." There is no ethnographic evidence that this kind of desertion ever took place; we have here a "what if?" story. That it is so in demand in the active repertoire of story-tellers indicates a desire to thrill to the situation of a young innocent, misjudged and ostracized.

What do you do in an utterly destitute position? This is the essential question posed in all versions of this absorbing mytheme. There is such variation in the way the young man (or young woman often enough) gets into trouble that the cause of the punishment does not seem to matter very much. What is important is that the cruelty and injustice of the world, and especially of those closest to us, be felt.

The second essential element is supernatural intervention to bring about the regaining of fortune. There may be help from a relative (often a grandmother, who makes sure you have fire) and there will be some self-discipline (note that the prince feeds his little slave before himself); but what we are looking for is the magic. In this case it is magical that eagles would remember the favours of the previous summer and now deliberately organize an escalating relief drop.

The third and crowning element of this coup d'état is the swing of the pendulum all the way to superfluity. Tate loves to see a good man thrive and amass riches. There never was so much blubber. The heaping up that ends this story is the Tsimshian way of expressing ecstasy. One should read the list of potlatch goods as pure poetry. It is repeated by Tate simply for the enjoyment of hearing the music of success.

The story of a Noble Prince, which deserted

There was a great Town
    of Giatwilgauz tribe[1]
        between Metlakaltha and Port Simpson
            where the great sand-bar at the front
                Kumalth'gho, her name.[2]
A great chief was there
    and his four brother-in-law.
        He has a young Prince
            his only son.

The Prince did not eat, but he chewing dried kidney fat, and he was sitting upon the top of his father's house, made arrows all the time. He has done it every day. And when the hump-back salmon arrived in the creeks, his father's tribe people went every where to catch salmon, and dried them for they Winter use. Also the Prince and his little slave went at the creeks in the big Bay and catch many hump-back salmon and bring home and unloaded it on the sand-bar at the front of the village,

and on the next morning
   them Eagles are gather there
     ate all them hump-back salmon.

He has done it in the whole summer and when the Eagles are fat their feathers are loose on the sand-bar and the Prince sent down his little slave to gather the Eagles' feathers, little slave went down and brought to his young master a many Eagles' feathers, and the Prince are very glad and he love to fed them Eagles with his salmon, because he wanted their feathers. He made arrows many boxes are full, and he used the Eagles' feathers to fasting them to the shaft,
     and so the arrows was very swift.

When the salmon was end the summer is past. Now the Winter came, and the people used up all their salmon, and all their kinds of food nearly gone. Then the Prince's father, the Chief, was always displease to his son because his son was feeding the Eagles in the summer while the salmon are arrived. Therefore great chief sent his wife to his four brother-in-law. He give her his advice
   let not one of my son's uncles pity on him
                   when he come
  starving and hungry to their houses
              for he was always feeding
  them Eagles in the passed summer.
             Let the Eagles fed him now,
  thus said the chief to his wife.

Therefore his wife went her elder brother's house she told him what her husband have said. The the elder brother said yes I will do it, she went in the second brother's, she told him what her husband adviced her. She went into the house of the thirth brother she told him the same thing then the fourth.

Every morning in this hard Winter the great chief said to his own nephews wake up and make fire. Then all the people into the house arose and seats it around the fire they ate little food,
  but his son sitting there
   chewing just little fat in his mouth,
    his parents give him
     no little food, because
      his father was angry.

On the following day that a Noble Prince lonely and he was disappointed for what his father and mother has done to him. Nearly every morning that his father have said to him now son go and feed them Eagles to you salmon the young man is crying, always.

    Therefore

        he went

            to his

                elder uncle's house.

Soon as he went in that his uncle said to his young men spread the mats at the side of the fire so they did now let my nephew sit on it. He said to his wife now feed my nephew so his wife took one dried good salmon and roast it by the fire then she cut it and she put it in a wooden dish then the young men

                                    layed the dish

before the Prince.   Then the uncle

                            arose up from his seat

and when the young Prince stretched forth his hand toward the dish to be took the roasted salmon,

                          then the chief took the dish fill

with roasted salmon away from him (Prince). He said,

                hoho if those who

                feed the whales last summer.

                with his salmon.[3]

Then he ate it with his wife.

    Therefore the young man is very much ashame for what his Elder Uncle has done to him. He went forth crying very sorry. On the next day he went again to his second Uncle's house soon as he entered his uncle said to his young men spread the mats along side the fire so they did. His wife roast a salmon and she cut put them in the dish and

            layed at the front of his nephew.

Before he (Prince) took salmon, his uncle took away from it and said

                hoho if this

                feeding Eagles

                should ate

                this good salmon.

    He ate it with his wife. Then the prince was very much ashame and went out crying. Next morning he went to his thirth uncle's house, and he sit down on one side of the fire, and his uncle's wife roasted the dry salmon. After she cut put it into the wooden dish and layed at the front of his nephew, before he take the salmon, his uncle took the dish away and said

hoho if this
feeding Eagles
would ate
this good salmon.

Then he went out crying bittery. He lay down on his bed and crying whole night.

On the next morning he went to his younger uncle's house. Soon as he entered younger uncle said to his men spread the mats along side the fire, then they did it as his order.

His young uncle
was crying
with his wife.

While his nephew was sitting there after they crying he said to his nephew I heard what those bad men has done for you, your Mother come round the other day and adviced us to treat you badly by your father the reason why they ill treated you. But I don't want to treat you that way.

After he talk to his nephew he said to his wife to roast the salmon. She did roasted and lay it at the front of him

but he did
not take it quickly lest they will take it away from him, but his uncle said ate them salmon my dear nephew so he take it and ate them and many kinds of food. In the mid night he went home he has a well satisfy.

Early on the next morning that his father said to his slave, Go out and order the people to move up to Naas then the great slave run out and shouting

move away
tomorrow
great tribe.

The people did move. They move it on the next morning. They left the chief son,

by the order of the great chief. (His young uncle's wife left one dry spring salmon and a pail of crab-berries and his little slave with him also ever burning fire and half little pail of greese.)

Now the people stard it,
they go to Naas.

When all the people went away, the prince gather old boards and ceder barks he build the house, small house. He just fed the little slave to a little salmon and crab-apples mixet with grease. Every morning very early, he went out and made some more arrows, and sat out side. It is very low water. Then he saw the Eagle screeched on the beach, some screaming. Then he call his little slave, Go down the beach and see why the Eagle screeching on the beach so he went down to where the Eagles are sitting. When he reached the place the Eagle flew away. Behold a trout lay on the beach.

Then he shouted
  with all his might and said
   a trout here
    my dear Master.

So the Prince said, Take it up here, then the slave carried up to the Prince, and the Prince ordered him to roast it. The slave roasted it. When she cook he said to his little slave ate them all. The slave ate them all.

Next morning very early the Prince went out again, he saw many Eagles screeching on the beach he sent his slave down the beach. Again he ran down and behold a large Bull-head was lying on the sand he shouted again and said a large Bull-head my dear Master. The Prince said take it up here. The slave took it up and they steamed it in the earth, the little slave ate. But the Prince did not eat any of it. They did so in several days, that the Eagle give them trouts and Bull-heads they dried them, then they had enough to eat.

On the next morning he went out and he saw Eagles are gather on beach and screeching. Therefore he sent his little slave down, he ran down again he look and behold a silver salmon was lying on the sand then he shouted again and said there is a silver salmon my dear. The Prince ordered him to take it, and he carried up.

The Prince
  cutting and roasted
   he ate a little.

They did so in several days and they dry them. Next day the Prince went out and he heard the Eagles' noise screaming on the beach. He sent down his little slave again, so the slave ran down and behold a large spring salmon lying on the sand. The slave shouted and said it a large spring salmon my dear. The Prince said take it, take it, so the slave took it up very heavy and while on his half way the Prince went down and helped him up to carried. Now the

Prince splitted to dried. They did this in many days his house was full with the dry fishes.

Another morning he went out as usually. He saw and behold many Eagles are way down the beach, he sent his slave down. Behold there was a great halibut lying on the sand he shouted and said a large Halibut my dear Master. The Prince said take it, but he cannot drag so he told to the Prince that he cannot drag it. The Prince went down himself and he dragged it up, he cut it and dried it.

Another morning the Prince went out he heard Eagles are screeching down the beach and there was a great many Eagles he saw. So he sent down his slave. And when the slave came there he behold a seal. Then the slave shouted, here is a great seal on the beach my dear Master. The Prince said take it, so the Prince went down and dragged the seal up to his camp. He split it and dried them. Now one house was full with all kinds of fishes *(wherefore the Eagles, restored the Prince salmon to feed them last summer, so they give him his foods)*. They did so in many days the seals are lying on the beach, and dried them all.

On one morning that the Prince went out, and behold many Eagles down the beach. He sent his slave down and when he came there Behold a large sealion lying there, he shouting as he could, here's a great sealion. He went in the woods and he took the ceder twigs and he twisted and join them together and when he finished he went down and tied the large sealion to shore, and when the tide rose he and the slave hauled up a shore by the tide. When the water turn and they lay on the beach, he cut it (Prince) and dried them. The other house was full with the dried seals, he have the other house for the sealion. The sealion are very large and they has much meat and fat. They did so in many days, and two houses are full with the sealions' meats and fats.

(Now the people   those who left him   are dying of starvation at Naas. No olachens   come up there   and no food for   the people.)

Another morning the Prince went out again, and there were a great number of Eagles are far out on the water.
They were
        flying ashore with
            a great whale,

and they land there, so the Prince and his slave went in the woods and took many ceder twigs and twisted in the whole day. They tied the great whale. On the next day they cut or chopped the blubbers they carried into one of a large house, they filled three houses because the whale is great

and they did so in several days.

Now they had ten great whales, they cutting six whales and four are remain on the beach. Therefore the Prince went out walking around

the whole village houses

are full with the blubbers

think over his uncle that was pitied him while his hungry. Therefore he called the seagull and ask her to rent her skin, so the seagull lent him, and he put it on, took a small piece of cooked seal

and he flew away to Naas.

And when he arrived there he saw many canoes trying catch olachens fish in their bag nets but could not catch many. The Prince fly over all them canoes trying to find out one of his relation among the canoes. At last he found his father's slaves in one of the canoe and he flew over it. A slave woman was sitting in stern while her husband and others working their nets. The seagull flew over her head he dropped down a piece of seal to her then the slave woman took it and she put it into her glove and she saw the seagull flew away straight down, until lose sight of it.

Now when they come home in the evening and while the people are all in beds the slaves' families are in one corner, and slave woman told her husband that the gull dropped the small piece of half dried seal where I am sitting into the canoe. Therefore the man has a little of seal, she also had little, and she give the whole to her child. The child were glad to have the seal, the child swallowed it and choked the child the child his almost die, because he swallowed all. The child's mother put her fingers into the child's mouth trying take the piece of seal that the child choking, but she can't for she has a short fingers. Therefore the chieftainess enquire

what the matter with

the child. The slaves says, We don't know. The chieftainess said bring the child by the light of the fire so that I might know. They did so. She said something hinder his breath, so the chieftainess put her long fingers and it reached down, she felt something and she took out a piece of boilded seal.

Behold a piece of seal.

Then she ask those slaves. Then she told it to her husband (The Chief). Therefore the chief ask them slaves where did they got the dried seal, so the Mother of the child told the chief how the gull dropped that piece of seal to her in the canoe at their fishing. The chief further more asking her, but where the gull went after she dropped down the seal to you, said he. The slave said

she went straight down.

Therefore the great chief said gather all the wise men and I will inquire them, so the great slave gather all the olden men, to the chief's house. He inquired them, they said some successful be on your son. So the chief wanted to sent canoe to-morrow to visit him. So they did.

On one morning they starded from there, and before evening, they arrived at the front of Port Simpson.

Behold the surface of the water

was covered with

grease. They paddled along. Now when they came to a place to where they left the Prince they reached there and they went ashore. Behold they see a great many bones on the beach and it smell the grease all over the sand at the front of the old Village. Them house are full of dried salmons, Halibuts, dried seals, sealions, blubbers of whales and four great whales on the beach.

They astonished and wonder

for what the Prince has done.

When the Prince saw the canoe coming to their town he went out and refused them to come ashore but

they ask him to have compassion on them,

but after a little while they landed. Then they ate dried salmons dried Halibuts seals meats sealions meats, Whales blubbers, and when they all satisfy the Prince command them and said don't told it to my father that I have plenty tell him that I am died long ago but I want you will be here two days eat as much as you can but don't take some pieces home with. Tell my young uncle that I wanted him to come home soon. I let him have one great whale that was lying on the beach, but I don't want my father and my mother will be here and also three of my elder uncles that mocked me in time of want, also all my father's people, but I desired all diferented tribes to buy all my provisions that you see in all these houses. Then he sent them back.

And when they arrived home at Naas, them slaves landed it there in the evening. They went up to the house of their Master. Then the chief asked them, is my son still live? says he. Yes was the answered he was still alive, moreover the slaves said your son that you left there has plenty no rooms for provision meats all kinds of fishes and fats of sea animals dried Trouts, salmons spring-salmon, dried seals, sealions and dried halibuts and many houses were full with Whales' blubbers, all them house were full with all kinds of meats and of fishes as well, and four great whales lying along the shore and
  great many boxes
    were filled with
      their greases
        and all the water's surface
          are covered with grease.
The Prince is success for these provisions, but he did not wanted to see you and his mother but only one his younger Uncle his order to come down to him and he will give him one great Whale. He did not want his three elder uncles and all your people, but he order me that he needs all different tribes to buy his provision.

Therefore the chief and his wife could not sleep in that night. Very early on the next morning that the chief said to his great slave,
  Order the people to return
    to our old Town where we left our Prince.
      Then we shall ask him for mercy
        lest we die here with starvation.
Therefore the great slave ran out and crying, Return to the old Town great tribe, and move by tomorrow, because Our great Prince are plenty in our old Village.

Early in the morning the chief and all his brother-in-law and all his people moves and they return from Naas to the old Village a sand-bar Town.

Then the elder Uncle's dressed his two daughters.
    Then they placed them on the box in his canoe,
        that he thought my nephew will marry them.
Then all them people paddled hard as they could. When they arrived out the front of P.S.
                Behold they saw
                        the grease
                                are covered the water,
            and one of those young lady
                stretched her hand
                    and dipped her finger to the grease
                    and ate it.
                But the younger Uncle
                            way behind
                                    them canoes.

One day at noon the Prince saw a great many canoes were approaching to them. The the Prince went out and ask them where are you people come from? They answered is your father here, and all your Uncles and your father's people. Again he asking who told you to come here? but they all speechless. He said again don't come ashore, or I will shots yours with my arrows, get away from here,
    and leave me alone with my starvation.
Then all the people pleading for him, so he had piteous to them, and ask them again but where is my younger loving Uncle? They said he was way behind there. Then the Prince did not allow to land until his younger uncle came. All those canoes were anchors at the front of the old Village. It was late in the evening that the younger uncle came. He landed there. But the Prince refused them to come ashore until next morning. He appoint one of the greater Whale and he give to him. His younger uncle gave his fair daughter to his nephew to be wife.

Next morning, Prince went out and call them ashore. When the canoe of his elder uncle near the shore those two girls dipped their hands to eat the grease that they saw on the water. Therefore the prince was very much ashamed. He did not wanted to see them.

He cut the half of the Whale and give the part to his father and the part to his elder uncle, and the cutting the other one whale and give the half to the second uncle and the half to the thirth uncle. Then he opened his storehouse of blubber he give one large whale's blubber to each man and each woman, he give small pieces to the children. He invited them to his house as a wedding feast. He love his wife. Then on the next day all different tribes were coming to buy some provisions. He bought Elk skins of many and some chiefs in different tribes sold him slaves, or a canoes, and prizely pearls, and many hundrens of scoreds of dried coon skins and sea-otters, marten's garments, dancing Blankets and of all kinds of goods.

And when he was riched above all the chief he invited all different tribes' chiefs and made a great Potlatch. And take his new name "Housh'dii." *(It means "to crave food.")* He given away many Elk skins, many slaves, and many marten's blankets, sea-otter's blankets, and dancing blankets, Elk-horn spoons, costly Pearls, and earrings of killer-whale's triangle teeths, and he became a great chief among these natives and his goods were increased, more and more. Again he made a great feasting, and he inviteds all chiefs more than he did before. When all the chiefs are in he took

ten costly coppers
ten large canoes
four scoreds and ten slaves
Elk-skins twenty scoreds
and sea-otter garments martens garment
dancing blankets, and many Elk-horn spoons.
also Elk-horn dippers and many costly pearls
and earrings of killer-whale's triangle teeth
and many boxes of greases
and crab-apples boxes mixted with grease
and of all kinds of provisions.

Now before he giving away all these, they took one of the costly copper, they cross it on his chest and take his new name, "Zunsh-'Lauk." *(It means "they had deserted him.")* After that, they proclamation to his new name. Then he took costly copper and he gave one to each chiefs and all the rests of good giving away also all the different Princes in every tribes received their gifts from him and all the chieftainess received

their horn spoons and horn dippers
    costly pearls
        earrings of triangle teeths
            and so on.

And as long as he live, them Eagles give him whales, sea-otters, sealions, seals, spring salmons, Halibuts, and all kinds of fresh fishes. His fame was spread all over the country in those days. He became so greater and greater until his life's end.
This is the end.

Notes

1 "Giatwilgauz tribe": Gitwilgyots, people of the kelp—a specific variety of wide-leafed kelp. "This name comes from a location at the mouth of the Skeena River where this kelp grows. The herring spawn on this plant which is then gathered" (Garfield 1939:176). The naming of the tribe has more to do with who is claiming the story than with any action in the story.

2 "Her name": The Tsimshian name given by Tate has been translated by William Beynon (in a manuscript) as simply "Place-of-Sand-Bar."

3 "With his salmon": This jingle, repeated twice below, is presumably the truly archaic core of the original Tsimshian story. At this point Tate is trying to find the English for a difficult bit of ironic word-play. Without worrying too much about the disjointed grammar, we can feel clearly enough the taunting sarcasm.

MYTHIC HISTORY

Revenge of the Mountain Goats

The schoolchildren of Glen Vowell Indian Day School just above Hazelton (as reported to Marius Barbeau in 1946) look out on Roche Deboule Mountain; to them it is Stekyawden, "Painted-Goat Mountain," and a sign "which they know means: 'Be Kind to Animals'" (Barbeau 1950:392; 1929:80). The one-horned mountain goat, who wreaks vengeance on a tribe that has been callous in their attitude to animals, and to mountain goats in particular, has become the well-known badge of the 'Ksan artists and performers of Hazelton. It is basically an inland Tsimshian (Gitksan) tradition. When Joshua Tsiyebeae dictated a version to William Beynon at Port Simpson in 1916 he made a point of saying that the crest was "not the privilege of the Larmawn (sea-coast) group" (Barbeau 1950:395).

This would be merely a moral tale, if it were not told as an important part of Tsimshian history. Reading between the lines, we detect the epochal significance: A civilization was destroyed by an avalanche because of ecological mismanagement.

The History of Mountain Goats feasting

Now while people lived at our own Village above the Skeena, which we named Park or Plain Village,[1] there was many hunters in those days, and they often went for hunteds and they succeeded to kill many beasts. Among those there were six brothers they were very handsome hunters than those hunters. They used to went in every falls for Mountain Goats hunts and they slew many goats at a time, but they don't get them just the goats' fatering kidneys and fat among intestines, and they left all their meats, and them Goats have distressed on this business for those hunters did not burn their bones or their meats in fire.

And those six brothers done the same thing in every falls.

Then on the next spring they went up on the same mountain, and they smote many goats as they did before,

and they caught a little kid or little Lamb and they brought down to their home.

Then
their children took down the little kid by the main River and cast
this little kid out of the River, and the poor little thing try to swim
ashore, and soon as the little lamb got ashore they (children) took
her again and threw her again into the water, and those children
was laugh when they see how funing that little kid while she
swimmed on the water. These children has done it many times.
Then this little kid catch cold. Then these children build a large fire
they lay down that little Lamb on one side of their fire to make her
warm and some of these children pushed this little Lamb on the
fire and all her furs was burned. They cast her again out the water
and they cried out for gladness.
Then some one
a young man
come down
to hear what these great noise means.
Then he went down to them children that sporting a little kid
and he caught that poor little kid out of them children and he rubs
her furs or wets furs with his hands to wipe the wet off from the
Lamb's wool.

This young man's name was "Common-Black"
and he guide her
away back their Village
and they reached at foot
of a high mountain.
Go on, supernatural, go on, say he.

And then they all forget what these children have done to that
little Lamb.

And before next fall was draw near, soon the messages coming
down to those Village,
and these messagers went to every houses
and invite every body man and women children and old, and they
told them
people that has just come down and build a new Village
at the foot of a high mountain yonder right on the plain
and the people of the Village received them messages gladly
and all the chiefs invited those messages to their houses as the custom was, and on the next morning these people has ready to go.

So they went and the messages was their conducted. They went on and on till the evening dawn. They went along on the plain as those messages told, and before evening fall they behold a large new building stood before them and they see the sparks flew up from the large house smoke hole,

and them messages overrun,

and these great multitudes of people stood on the plain at little further off from the front of a large building waiting for the other messages come to meet them, and when the other message came up and meet them, then they went towards the building and before the multitudes went into the building, they all came forth from the building

> and dancing
>> without the house
>>> as the custom
>>>> when the chief invite some other people.

Those people that was dancing wear on them a Mountain Goat's head of their head dress, and Mountain Goat's skins their blankets, and soon after dancing those multitudes of people went into it, they have a sang a song as the custom, and when all the multitudes in

> then one of the young man came along,

and went

towards a young man name "Common-Black" and this young man ask "Common-Black" my friend I want have you with me, and we will sat beyond that post there. And they went together. And as they sat behind that post, then the chief began to dance and they sing a first song of chief dance and a beautiful mountain stood in the middle of a large building at the interior, and at the end of a first song, then they begun to the next song.

And when the next song stard it behold a Mountain Goat
> coming along side a mountain
> with one horn on his head

and coming down from the top of that mountain, he leap down along until he reached down the foot of that mountain
> and all the congregation of people

says he looks like

a real

Mountain Goat.[2]

And while the last song was going on that the Mountain Goat
leaped before the congregation
                              and kick the front
                                            he leaped on
          one side
                    and kicked it again,
then the building earth floor was break down
    and all them congregation of people
        was destroyed
          along side
            of a high mountain.

Only one young man name "Common-Black" was saved, he was
saved at the foot of little spruce tree behind the house post, but
now it become little spruce tree way up above a high mountain
side.

No way for him to escape, for the rocks had very steep above
him and below and every side. He began to look down below on
the next morning and he to crying for fearing, but his friend lied
down and had a good sleep by his side till the sun raised up high
in the sky.
And the young man "Common-Black" wept often, then the
young man that was slept by his side wake up from his sleep and
said, What is the matter you my friend? Then the fearful man
"Common-Black" said it's because all my people was slidding
down by these mountains steep side and choked, and I had no
way to escape from this steep place. Then the young man that was
sleep told him, did you know who invites you people? The man
"Common-Black" says no. Then the young man that was sleep said
          the Mountain Goats has done it
                              because
they was distressed for what you people hunts them every years
and killed them but the hunters
                              don't took them to their home
          but they leave them
                    among the mountain and they were
decay the bones of them Mountain Goats was scattered all over the
mountain instead them hunters burn the Mountain Goats' meats
skins bones and all.

So the Goats' vengeance was great to you
people.

And you are the man
   that take pity on me
      while the children of thy people
         throwed me out the river
            last spring
and you kindly lead me away back your Village for freedom.
                                                      So   I
will free you out this steep side mountain.
                              Be not afraid
                                          you shall
get down safely
               I shall let you have my blanket.
                                       And "Common-
Black" had a little refresh for what his friend has said to him yet he
still fear.
   And the young Goat had on his skin
                              I shall show you
                                          what you
have done
         before he leap and he say
                        on the thumb!
and he (young Goat) turn his head towards the gulf of a steep
rock, and leaped again and say
                        on the sand!
                           and so on till he went
further down, then "Common-Black" lose sight of him.
   Again "Common-Black" began to cried out and weep for he lose
sight of his friend and sat down behind the little spruce and while
he was bitter cry, behold a young Goat coming down above him
along from the top of a high slipping mountain. And he came to
where the fearing man, and said
                        you see is a dangerless thing
         you might try it.
Then the poor trembling man have the young Goat's garment and
put it on himself with a very fearful. The young Goat have said to

him do not so fearful you would have no harm. A young Goat give his friend his good advised. Before you leap and you shall offer two words is this

            on the thumb!

                      and when you leap

on one side then you shall offer one is this

                   on the sand!

                          then you

might offer these two words all along your way until you got down safely.

     And when you get down safely, then chose or pick out your relation among those corpses and put them in good order. When you've done it, as many as you want to live, then you leap over them corpses until they relife. You shall leap over them at four times, and you shall hang my blanket on one of the tree branch below, and you shall go home with thy relation and your people. Thus said the young Goat to his friend "Common-Black."

     Then soon as "Common-Black's" friend speech was ended his stard it away. Before he leap down he said as his friend command him and said

            on thumb![3]

Then he jumped (he wear the young Goat's skin) and his foot sticked to rock as ever. Then turned his head another way. Before he leaped he offered another word

                   on the sand!

                     his foot sticked.

Then he went down along with fearless. He soon got down at foot of a high steep mountains, and he gather the corpses of his relation and he put them in good orders as his friend Goat commanded him. Then he jumped over them corpses four times. Then all them that bodys was resurrection. Then the young man named "Common-Black-Of-Raven-Feather" hunged his friend blanket on one of the branches. Then they all went home.

     On the following day that the young man gather all his relation they went at foot of a high steep mountain to where the Goats' bones layed and they heaped them together and burned them all and they went round to burned the bones of Goats and their meats also their fur or wools skin as well.

     So the people in those days did not scold them animals of any kind, and burned them animals' bones or meats, they did not left the animals' bones on the hill. The story is when the hunts burned the bones or meats, then them animals had got better from his sickness. As long as the bones lie waste on the ground and the beasts' sickness grew worse and worse and they cannot be cure. This is the story told by the young Goat to his friend at behind little spruce tree at the side of a slipping rock mountain.

This is the end.

These are the words of a Goats sing while kicked down the people in his dancing tune.

> *Oh yi yi yea ha'a yi yi yea ha'yi yeh a a a'a*
> *On one side of a high mountain*
> *That it layed my hoof a'a'a'*
> *Because Prince of Mountain Goat*
> *Kicked down on the side mountain.*

Notes

1 "Plain Village": This is Tate's English rendering of "Dumlakam"—the cradle of the Tsimshian, the Temlaham of Barbeau's *The Downfall of Temlaham* (1928), said to be near the present Hazelton, B.C.

> What is Temlaham today, what is it to us, who live on reserves conceded by the Ramkseewah, the White Man? A legend of the past, a barren stretch, two miles below Hazelton on the Skeena, a place we still visit at times, when we are sad at heart. Our people once lived there, lived happily for an age. So we are told, so we believe...The only thing left for us to cherish now is its memory, the memory of its unearthly beauty (Barbeau 1928:243-44).

2 "Like a real Mountain Goat": Up to this point, the mountain-goat hosts have disguised themselves and gone through the form of a potlatch with theatrical landscape backdrop and masked "realistic" dancers—only too real, as it turns out.

3 "On thumb!": Charles Mark of Gitseguekla, telling this story to Marius Barbeau in 1923, explained: "As the goat went down the mountain, sometimes there happened to be no place to jump. Then he would say, 'The-little-thumb.' Then a piece of rock would jut out" (Cove and MacDonald 1987:250). In the version of Paul Dzuis of Gitanmaax, as well as saying "thumb-sticking-out," the anxious young man added "ledge of rock!" just to make sure (Cove & MacDonald 1987:247). The other safety net catchphrase "on the sand!" is not mentioned in the above stories.

The Tsimshian Descend to the Sea

You might say that there is no flood here, certainly no "world's flood" as we would envision it from Genesis. There's just the overflow from a lake when a water monster surfaces. Ah, but this flooding triggers events which change everything. It ultimately brings about the migration of upper Skeena civilization to the sea coast. The lake "whale" is the presiding diety over the shamanic rebirth of two brothers, one of whom survives to be the national leader. It needs a great shaman to be able to see in his mind's eye such an unknown thing as the halibut. He must be toughened by utmost hardship and be victorious over all other shamans. Then he can lead his starving people with prophecy of the rich rewards from the new technology of sea fishing.

Can we take this story as the Coastal Tsimshian's mythologizing of a dim racial memory of an origin in the Interior? We get little expert help on this question. Boas certainly thought the Tsimshian "recent intruders on the coast" (1916:872), but he refrained from using this legend as evidence for the idea of an actual prehistoric migration.

The History of the World's Flood

Almost the end
            of our grantfathers' lives
                        at Skeena

(as I mention on the other history,[1] which we named Park or Plain
Village)

and most of the people
                        was very clevers
                                    they are handsome hunts
brave in war
            and so on.

So, on that days some hunters wents away from their homes
toward the sun rise. Soon they got along side a great Lake which
they named "Very Oldest Lake." *(This was the Lake of Skeena*

River.) As soon as they (hunters) got there then the waters of the great Lake was became swelled then overflowed. These great Lake and the Skeena River was flood, at that time almost the Villages of Skeena was swift by the currents of a stream. Then those hunters look and they Behold a great whale forth on the Lake above the surface of the water, so the water of a great Lake was swelled before a very large Whale was forth on the Oldest Lake water. And those hunters names it a coverts with fish-gills or four in a row horns over the body like the Grampus back horn it stood near the spout hole of Grampus,[2] and while the great whale or Shark went down then the waters decreased.

And then another years was come that two brothers of that same Village starded off and they went up to that Oldest Lake to get them a supernatural powers. They got there, then the elder one went out into the water. As soon as the water reached above his knees, then he sinked down to the bottom of that Oldest Lake. Then the water swelled again as it swelled before while the large Whale forth, and his brother remained ashore he saw the waters rised up higher and also the Skeena River was flood again than it was before, for the water of Oldest Lake was swelled up higher than ever.

And as soon as the man sink down

          he saw a large house
at the bottom of the sea.

There he went into it and no one was in there but a large fire light in the center of a house and he himself sat down on the mats on the side of fire.

While he sat there a while

       that door open suddenly, and

            behold
lightning flashing

     come it into the door

         and it is done it
four times.

     Then the thunder rolling

         it done it four times

it is a very terrible
                    thunder rolling
                            and it ceased
after four times.
                Then the hail was began
                                and it's very fearful
        hailing.
Soon afterwards, that the large Grizzly Bear come forth from out of
the wooden carved vail in the middle of the rear of the house. The
Grizzly Bear come towards the man that sat down on the mat at
the side of a large fire. The Grizzly Bear stood before him, and said
take me and open my back. This said
                            the Grizzly Bear, to the man.
    Then he did it,
                and it was became a carven box,
and the Thunderbirds came forth from out the wooden carved
vail, came toward the man. Thunderbird said to him
                                    take me
and put me in
            thy box
                    and the man took it and put it into his
Grizzly Bear box.

    Thunderbird was a Drum
        and lightning was his red ochre
        and a living Ice forth out from the wooden carved vail,

and after a little while behold a very large animal come into the
door which they named in those days "Both-Ends-Mouths" and
came towards the man and stood before him take me and put me
into thy box, also Cuttle-fish dab came in she went towards the
man, which it said take me and put me in thy box. That man took
them both and he put them into his Grizzly Bear box. At last the
living Ice came in (it is Hail, it was a beating stick) she also went
towards the man which also said take me and put me in thy box.
Then the man took her and put it in his carven box.
                Yet still no
                living person
                could be seen
                in that house.

Then he stard it homeward, and the living Grizzly Bear said to him your name shall be call "On-Mouth" or "Both-Ends-Mouth." The man went ashore of that lake with Grizzly Bear walked by his side.

And then the man been away down the depths of the Oldest Lake his been there quite a long while. So it was his brother waiting for him his brother waiting him since the water was decreased from swelled and overflowed the Oldest Lake and during he is waiting still until the twenth days, and he was hungry he sat himself at the foot of a large spruce tree, and died there with starvation.

Then the mardens come and eat him, the mardens eats all his meats and consumed it. But only his bare bones was left to where he was sitting.

As soon his brother "On-Mouth" come ashore from the Lake he look and behold his brother skeleton layed at the foot of a large spruce tree. Then his brother just been from out up the water he was wept to see his brother bare bones was layed there. He come towards it, and try to heal him. He took up the earth and rubbed it with his hands to make his brother bare bones became meats again. Then his brother's bare bones soon became a human flesh. But he has no skins so he took a small roots to make him nerves, and "On-Mouth" or "Both-Ends-Mouths" dancing around with his supernaturals power, and he took up the common moss and rubbed it over flesh, and it become skins, and make him alive again.

And he make his brother also a shaman.[3]

And he give his name was "Devoured-by-the-Mardens." And "On-Mouth" caught them mardens that eats his brother meats and put them living mardens at inwards of his brother, and a vessel of blood to be his Supernatural Power.

They went back home with this living Grizzly Bear walked down with them. Soon they got to their home. "On-Mouth" can cure any kinds of disease, or he can healed those person died sudden.

Then all them supernaturals powers into rocks heard that "On-Mouth" had a great really supernaturals powers, trying to kill him. However, "On-Mouth" knew it and he was ready to fight with them. As soon as some one of them supernaturals or any shamans come in secret to kill him, then the shaman "On-Mouth" sent out his supernatural it was "Both-End-Mouths" and "Cuttlefish" killed those fellow trying to murdered his master. Or if any shaman come through the water then "Both-Ends-Mouths" and "Cuttle-fish" went into the waters and destroyed them. Or if some shamans with their supernaturals power come upon land and the Grizzle Bear fought with them and destroyed it. Or if some supernaturals come up and flight through the air, then Thunderbird and lightning with hails destroyed them. So it is no way to those supernaturals from all parts of the world to kill this shaman "On-Mouth."

At last two great shamans come along in their canoe. (Those shamans we call mans half-women or half-men.)[4] Two of them in one canoe. Then "On-Mouth" sent down his two supernatural powers that is "Both-Ends-Mouth" and "Cuttlefish." Then those two shamans sent up their supernatural power also.

It is blood.

So the supernatural of "On-Mouth" was killed in the blood, both of them died, "Both-Ends-Mouth" and also "Cuttle-fish," and also to shaman "On-Mouth" death.

And only his brother "Devoured-by-Mardens" went forth and sent down his supernaturals, that is "Blood" and "Mardens." He slewed those two shamans that was in the canoe, and he took his brother Grizzly Bear box and his brother Thunderbird Drum and lightning and hails. His brother "On-Mouth" went home to the bottom of the Oldest Lake. Then "Eat-by-Mardens" was alone he was conquered to all them supernaturals all round.

And many years has passed by that the famine was so great in the land. At winter, then the people of "Devoured-by-Mardens" come up to him, and they said you are really supernatural power, it is good for you have try to have some provision for us. So this shaman lied down on one side the fire he ask his friends to covering him with ceder bark mat, and he stard his supernaturals' song.

These are the words of "Devoured-by-Marden's" dancing
song

> *My devours supernatural*
> *To others Shaman*
> *Large light-ning in the air when they took me in*
> *Large supernatural at olderest Lake.*

Before he stard to sing and
  Thus he said,
    ever-living fish, ever-living fishes,
  my supernatural told me
    were ever-living fishes
      was now.
So we must go   to where them fish was   lest we died with starvation   if we still abide   in this old village   then we shall die in
starving.

So then all his relation stard on the next day. They got into their
canoes and descendeds the river. They had a long board in their
canoes. They tights those four canoes together and they put that
long board across them canoes. There the shaman lay down on the
plank, which was painted with red, and covered himself with mat.
Those four canoes where the shaman layed went before them, and
many canoes went behind them. He said always along the way the
same words, is this

  ever-living fish, ever-living fishes

went down the river farther on. Just only a word the shaman, said
ever-living fish, ever-living fishes. He has told his people where
ever-living fish was, he point with his finger way down the river,
until they got down at the mouth of Skeena River. Then the
shaman say,
  way out the sea.
They paddle along and soon they got between Stephens Island
where a good place for camp is a sandy shore. The shaman said
this is the place that my supernatural power was appoint to me.
Then they all camped on the sandy shore.

Shaman said to his people go and had and bring down bent
branches from red ceders or yellow ceders. Then his people went

and brought bent branches. More over the shaman said make hooks out of it, and they did so. They obeyed the shaman.

Let your women make a fishing lines out of red ceder bark.

So them women make a fishing lines. They measured at sixty fathoms in length of each fishing lines. Moreover he said to them women go and bring down spruce small roots and split it, and they did as the shaman had said to them.

Then he (shaman) also said to them men
    go down when the tide is very low
        and you can find a differend fishes beneath the rocks
            with eight legs and round head
                her eyes on her necks
                    its dab, bring them up
                        and tight it on your wooden hooks as your bait.
The men did as the shaman said, and while they got finish it that the shaman said launch out your canoes and forth for fishing. So they went.

The shaman stood on the beach and point out. The shaman wears all his supernaturals cloths. "Devoured-by-Mardens" put on a bearskin for his garment wear on his dancing apron and his bear-claws was his crown and he paint his face with red, mixed with charcoals. He also have rattles in his both hands and soft Eagle feathers scattered all over his body. Thus shaman said again

        ever-living fishes, ever-living fishes.

Then all his people have to say the same, ever-living fishes, ever-livng fishes. The shaman has offered three or four time repeated. Now they went. The shaman stood there on the beach still, and point. He say go little farther out, launch out into the deep and you shall find them. So did they went. Now the shaman still stood on the beach, and said pull up your fishing lines. They hauled their lines up. All their hooks are well filled with halibut
    and those people afraid
        to have those because
            as a new things to them.
                They did not knowed
                    before.

Finally the shaman told them people to let them have those halibuts into their canoes. They brought them ashore and cooked them halibut, and "Devoured-by-Marden" ate it first. *His supernatural Power told him that halibut is good for food, so those starving people have them halibut to be their provisions.* Now they had well satisfys, every days with ever-living fishes, as the supernatural powers have told "Devoured-by-Mardens." *This is the first visitation of Skeena River people at salt water, and they first known to them how to caught halibut in the bottom of a depths of the sea.*

They build
    a new Village there.
        They return not
            up to Skeena River.

Notes

1 "The other history": Tate sent this story to Boas on 18 March 1905 with the previous story, "Revenge of the Mountain Goats." In doing so he has provided two alternative explanations for the "downfall of Temlaham." The setting is taken to be the upper Skeena near Hazelton, but the site of the "Oldest Lake" has not been guessed at.

2 "Grampus": another name for the killer-whale or blackfish, but the lake creature described in this story is a multi-finned, many-gilled, supernatural killer-whale. In his Tsimshian language line Tate uses the word which is translated usually as "sea-monster."

3 "Shaman": Traditionally, a shaman has to be reduced to a skeleton, and then fortified with special strengths. That he is restored to life means that he can restore others. Marie-Françoise Guedon has cited this passage as "one of the prototypes of all Tsimshian shamans" in her article "Tsimshian Shamanic Images" in *The Tsimshian* (Margaret Seguin, ed. 1984:193).

4 "Half-men": Boas uses the word "hermaphrodite" here (1916:348), adding a footnote that "probably homosexuals are meant" (1916:862).

Eagle Clan Story

This is one of the basic narratives of the Haida-Tsimshian world. Marius Barbeau got it from old Chief Mountain in 1927 at Kincolith on the Nass River (1950:17), and William Beynon got a Kitimat version from Edmund Patalas in 1947 (1950:81), and others (Barbeau 1953:34; 1961:8, 25).

In its present form it belongs to a Tsimshian Eagle clan family, tracing its family tree back to a princess from a Haida Eagle clan village. Deaksh survives the conflagration of her village, and later the gale which blows her canoe to the mainland. She found a good home among the Tsimshian, and became the first lady of a dynasty. Some of her children returned to the Queen Charlottes, and the story implies that this established good diplomatic relations between the Haida and the Tsimshian. This is a myth.

Do not expect a tight plot from a crest story of this kind. Crests are picked up in the course of much meandering. The interest is in the crests themselves, and the repetitions are meant to impress the validation stories upon the memories of family members.

The history back-from-sea-to-shore

A good many years ago in a certain Village which we called Zegwa,[1] there was a chief and his wife to which they had two children one boy and girl, and the boy's name, Ashdilthda *(that means "Back-from-sea-to-shore")* and the girl name Deaksh *(which means "Signify")*.

So on the next day, the young prince went forth and call together his three companion and they took a canoe and out up to river Zegwa for Trout fishing as they used to be in every Spring's time. And the young prince seat at the bow of his canoe and two others seated in the middle, and one seated at the stern. And they went up the river until their arrived the place where fishing ground was, and soon the young prince look down into clear water that he saw many Trouts coming under their canoe and the young prince took up his harpoon with two sharp points on one end *(this is the pole they used)*

And this young prince wear on his costly hat, this hat is very pricely *(we named "Hat of Cormorant")* it covers with pricely pearls,

and no one wear the hat same as this.

only this prince,

as a sign to his relation.[2]

And now he spear good many Trouts, at last the large Trout come up again and try to spear her also. Before he spear that, his costly hat fell and the Trout gone and he mist it.

And again he placed his hat on rightly, he looked down once more, that he saw a large Trout come slowly then he took up his harpoon again and his ready to spear and before he spear that his costly hat fell off and he losed sight of it the Trout gone. And then he put on his hat rightly again, and look down then he saw another large Trout come again and he try to spear and before he spear then the Trout gone, for his hat fell and losed sight of it.

And then he was wroth and took off his costly hat and tore to piece and cast it into the water and sinked down. The stern-man took long pole and hooked up the costly hat, and stern-man put behind him in the canoe stern.

Then the prince say let us camp ashore for it toward evening and they camp at root of a large spruce tree as they used to camp in every spring as passed by. They build the fire and ready to roast some Trouts for their supper, and soon the Trout was cooked, then the partners went and carry skunk cabbage leaves, and spread on the ground then and placed roasted Trout over it as a dish,

and immediately

the frog

was leaped on the cooked Trout,

and the frog was seated on it. Then the prince's wroth was kindrend against the frog, so he took the frog and cast it into the fire, and the frog leaped out from off the big fire. Then again he took the frog and cast again once more into the fire. Then the poor thing trying to escape from him but the poor frog was in vain, for the young man strongest than her. Then at last the frog was died into the fire

and then one of these young prince
partnership take away

106

the scorching frog, and threw the carcase away, secrets, in the bush. Then their have supper.

They lie down and slept and on the next morning very early the prince said to his companion let's go home. They launch out their canoe, and starded it homeward, and when they all aboard to their canoe, they paddle away little farther off from their camp, that behold the young woman coming down the beach behind them, and she cried out and said, sirs, will you take me along with you. (The woman blacking her face with charcoals for her moarning.) And then these young men turn back to her, for the young prince has very favours of this young woman beauties. And this prince jump out from his canoe to take her and he stretch out his hand to embrace her, then the woman vanished away from his sight, only the frog leaped away from him.

And he went down to his canoe and paddle away from it, and when they went little farther off, they heard a cried behind them and said

     sirs, will you take me

               along with you

then these young men

           ceased their paddle

                and they look back,

and the prince look on the beauty of her, and he said to his part-ner let's turn back and take her along, so the canoe turn back towards her. Then they arrived ashore to where she's coming down the beach. Then the prince out off his canoe and walk up to the woman and he stretch forth his both hands to embrace her

                       then

she vanished again,

        just the frog leap

               away from him.

And he went down to his canoe and off away again.

They paddle away farther that the woman come down the beach and she cried out and says (sirs) will take me along with you? then these men ceased to their, they look back they saw a good looking woman coming down. The prince[3] said that they might turn back and

     take her so they turn back and reached the place to where she coming down then the prince out, and went to her to meet her. The woman coming down, and the prince went up quickly and he put forth his hands to embrace her then she vanished away from him, just frog leap off from him, and he went down to his canoe and out again they paddle away hart and when they went on further off, they heard a crying behind them and she said (sirs) will you take me along with you? Then the Prince answered her. Oh no, lest you vanish away from us. Thus said the young Prince to her, and she offered again once more, yet they paddle away hardly as they could away from her. And so the woman has said to them (sirs) will you listen to what I've say to you? So they cease their paddle and listen,

As you went along there
    when you arrive that point yonder
        that your Prince fell back and die there.
            and when you reach another point
                then one of them that sit in the middle of the canoe
                shall die also,
                    and before you arrive at beach of your Village
                        that the next man shall die also
                            And your steerman
                        soon as he finish
                    his story to your people
                is what happen to you
            and he shall die.
        Thus said the woman to them.

And paddle away along from her they laugh at her to scorn ha, ha, you will soon die yourself.

They paddle away. Soon they reached the same point that woman foretold them. Then the Prince (or Ashdilthda) fell back and died,

and his partnership
    paddle away
        with weeping
            and sorrowful.

And while they paddle along with weeping that one of them that sitting in the middle of the canoe felled back and died also,

and

two of them left was paddle along, and before they reach the shore of their Village that the next of them fell back and died also, and the steerman remain, and arrived at the shore, and the crowds of people coming down and question him for what happen to those deaths, and the steerman did not say a word to them till he went up to his father's house, yet the people still question him is what happened to them. As soon as he got in his father's house, and the crowds followed him in and the house full with the village people, then he (steerman) commence his story.

Yesterday while we arrived at the fishing ground and our Prince (or Ashdilthda) spears good many trouts and before we go to our camp, he look down (the prince) and he behold a large trout coming along and immediately took up his harpoon and ready to spear the large trout that his hat fell to forward to his eye, and the trout gone. His costly hat fell several times at in time his ready to spear and the trouts gone and at last he was wroth and took off his costly hat and tore it to piece and he cast it into the water and when I saw the hat sinked down slowly then I took my long pole and hook her up and I place her behind me into the canoe at the stern, and the evening dawn we camp at the foot of a large spruce tree and then we build a large fire ready to cook our supper, and we roast some of the trouts. Soon the trouts cooked and we went for skunk cabbage leaves and as we spread them on the ground as our dish then we placed the trout we roasted on it and as soon we sit around then a frog leaped on it. And our prince (or Ashdilthda) was angry against the frog and he took her and cast it into the fire and the frog leaped out from the fire. The prince took her again and cast her into the fire. The frog try to escape from him but she can't, then again the frog try to leap out from the fire. Then the prince took a long pole and pressed her into the fire and the frog try to escape from him but she can't he pressed hard till the poor thing died and scorched and,

steerman said,

then I took secretly and I threwed it away in the bush, and then our fire almost out, we lied down and slept in our camp until the next morning. And soon we have our breakfeast and when we through

breakfeasting our prince said that might back home
early so we stard homeward, then while we paddly
away from our camp we heard a screaming or crying behind us.

      Thus said the steerman.
      while the people crowd round about him
      in his own house,
      more over says he (steerman)

We behold a young woman standing on the beach
of our camp she blacking her face signs of
moarning with charcoals and she said sirs will you
take me along with you in thy canoe? so our prince
said let's turn back and fetch her with us, so we
turn back to her then we reached a shore, and our
prince forth from the canoe he went to her, and he
stretched forth his to embrace her, for he was
favoured to her, she was also of a goodly coun-
tenance and very beautiful to look upon so it is the
prince put forth his hands to embrace her, and she
was vanished away from our sights and the prince
saw only frog leaped away from him. This was
done to us at three times, and we paddle from our
camp unheed her words, then she cried out more
and more after us. At last she said sirs just cease for
a while till I told you some thing, then we could
cease our paddly and she said just listen to what I
say, said she. When you reach that point yonder
and your prince fell back and die there, and when
you reach that other point farther on, that one of
that sitted in the middle shall die there, and again
the next shall die also before your arrived at home,
and your steerman as soon finish his story to your
people.

      Thus said the steerman,
      and he fell back and died.

Then all the people of the village move and they took death's bodies and buried them.

Then on the next morning an "Age's-Woman" by her name, she very old, and she live at the end of the village and she went to the chief house the father of the young prince that has died at later on, and she said ("Age's-Woman") gather all the people of the village, and the Chief sent and invite all his people and when all the people come into the chief's house "Age's-Woman" now dear people I have a dreamed last night, and all the people very anxious to know the "Age's-Woman's" dreamed, so her people question her for what her dreamed. Then she say I had a very bad dreamed. And she said to her Chief which lost his young son, you must dug out the earth in the middle of your house or in the center dug out deep, and put thy only daughter into it, so the Chief command to dug out the earth and when they done dug it out they put costly Copper first and carven garments it's very costly also and many other properties. This costly Copper they put it on each side of the dugged out earth, first costly garments of sea-otters and garments of mardins and Chief garments dance and many elk skin

and

young girl

went down into it.

Then they covering the dugged earth with planks of boards and fill over the plank.

And "Age's-Woman," soon she knew the Princess Deaksh covering with earth that she said ("Age's-Woman") I dreamed and I saw the fire fell out from heaven, and consume this Village.

I saw,

said she,

a fire fell on the top of that mountain yonder

as she point

the top of that same mountain,

Behold a little fire brand fell down on the top of the mountain and it streaming down quickly as the waters down from the top of a mountain

so it is with the fire.

The fire went around the Village and then the water beneath the Village burnt as an oil.

Then the Village people would not escape from it. They all burned and consumed.

Only that young princess that was hide in the dugged earth was save, and also "Age's-Woman" hide herself in to the earth. And Princess Deaksh (or "Signify") heard the noise of fire

pass over her into the earth.

And

while the noise was ceased, then she heard the voice of very "Age's-Woman" coming down crying. And she (Deaksh) heard that "Age's-Woman" moarning song. For she ("Signify" or Deaksh) knew very "Age's-Woman" voice

> wept
>> above her
>>> in the earth.

This is very "Age's Woman" moarning song
* it above her   while she was   in earth*
*   "I just gather the bones of my dearest my dearest."*

And after little while, then she ("Signify") heard also another voice coming along, so she pushed away the cover off from her. Behold the chieftainess coming she (chieftainess) has a cane in her hand the cane has a living frog at low end of the cane, and the living person on the top of living frog, and the living Eagle on the top end of the cane and the chieftainess wear on her large roots hat paint with green

> she walk
>> slowly,
>>> along,

then she talked with very "Age's Woman," she call (chieftainess) very "Age's Woman,"

don't you know

that Ashdilthda

cast my only child

into the fire

so I burned up this village.

And after she repeated her tune three times then she put her child's name on her moarning song

on the last line

of her moarning

is this

> Zilaagonish.

That's the name of that frog was cast into the fire by the Prince while on their way to fishing trouts.

And now while the chieftainess went away the girl "Signify" (or Deaksh) come forth from her hiding place, the girl knew very well the moarning song of that chieftainess just passed by, and soon she forth from dugged she look around her with her deep sorrow, she saw no body save consumed village. Then she went along she don't know which way to go to and stard it away. Before she went she put on her garments of sea-otter and garments of mardin, and carven garments or chief's dancing garment and then she put in order those costly copper and all elkskins she leave it in her hiding place. Then she went off, with her moarnfully, and then she offered her own custom her own moarning song.

This is the words of Deaksh's mourning song when she went along the way as soon as she leave the village after it consumed by the fire

1

When he went to spears dearest sir, al-as
When he went to spears dearest sir, al-as

2

Then fell his hat of Cormorant dearest sir, al-as
So the village of Zegwa sir destroyed, al-as

3

So the village of my dearest sir destroyed, al-as
So the village of Zegwa sir destroyed, al-as

4

Then the glittering garment went forth, al-as
So the village of Zegwa was destroyed, al-as.

And is this song that she had sang.

And she went along the way in the desert crying along the way. She went on and on till she reached along side a large Lake and while walk around the Lake that she behold

a beautiful garment

spread before her on the ground

                    it glittering as the stars of heaven.

    This garment is full

            with the foam

                of living persons.

(And she had this glittering garment in her moarning song.) She wept all along her way, then she passed by that garment, and while she went on around the Lake

             suddenly she heard

a great noise out of the water

          into Lake

its rolling as a thunder rolling

         so she look and behold,

   supernatural Halibut

    coming up

      on the water

        as a house carven

         (and she took it her moarning song).

Then she passed by on her way, she struggle along on her way, yet she's weary and fainted on account of her starvning and her voice almost lost for her weakness. And by and by she (Deaksh) coming down on the other side of seashore and she saw a fire burning under the root of one spruce tree. Then she went towards it with her weakness

     her garments are almost gone

      on account of her long journey.

And she sat down by the fire her back was against the fire

     and this fire after burned

      of one death princess body

       in the next town.

     And the chief and chiefess only daughter

      was death and burned there.

And while the wandering Princess (Deaksh) sat by the corpse fire and warmed herself there was a canoe coming with four people in it,

   which they saw a young princess sat by the fire and they passed on towards the village over the other side, and they bring news to the people of village, they say that they saw a young princess sat by the corpse-fire over there,

          and all the people controll and they

114

said that the princess became life again. So the Chief and his wife went over to see is what happen there and they arrived on the beach behold a princess sat down by the fire. They come ashore quickly as they could and the Chief and his wife

came towards fire
then all the company, and chiefess embraced the girl and she (Chiefess) asked the girl, what is your name? The girl said that her name was "Signify'" and so on,

    and that
      the same name
        of the Chiefess only daughter
          just burned on that fire
            to where this wandering princess.

Then the chief and his wife and his people took with them to their home with gladness and made a great feast to his people for his death girl was alive again, a little ago. And so the young Princess live with her new parent,[4] and she been there for a long while and her new parent love her so much. And her parent make her married to one of his nephew.

And in the next summer while straw berries was riped and all the young women stard out for to picking straw berries to a certain of the Islands away little farther out their village, then all those young women got out of the canoe to one of those Island, and the young princess was left alone in the canoe. And when all those party began to picking straw berries that this princess was alone in the canoe starded and she went out to go on to the next Island. And while she on her way that immediately a great stormy southwest wind blew her away, off and off. The strong winds drives her canoe, away from her new home again. And then she soon arrived at the midst of a great sea which she unknown. And while she sang her moarning song that she sing when she wander away in desert after fire consumed her own father old Village, then she looked
  and behold
    a great thing
      looks like a large Eagle
        came forth on the water
        with ten small Eagles
          covers the head of a large one.

Then she drivens on and on until she reached at little outside our old town Metlakatla. She reached at the shore of Kitwilgeowatz tribe,[5] and the chief of Kitwilgeowatz have her to his house and married her. Soon and she bare him three sons and two girls, she has a happy new home again.

The Chief was married her has five wifes beside her, and so he has six wifes altogether. And on the next day, that old wife of this chief was quarrel with this princess, for the chief love her most. And the old woman said to this young princess

                    The chief has not
intended to married you.
                    You are driven away
                              by the south-west
on thy way to picking straw berries
                    you are slave of Haida.
Thus said the old chief wife to her, Deaksh.

And then her children grew up. The elder son used to hunter and they became rich on the strange land, and these boys make a big Potlatch to all the Zimsheans tribe, and have their names.
        The elder son have his name Ashdilthda,
        second was name Younansh,
        thirth Gumkagan,
        and the girls name
        first Lukshmankash,
        second Alulalth,
        and Sha-gabin.
Then they had another large feasting, and new, Ashdilthda make a head dress Cormorant cover with pearls *(as the old Ashdilthda wear it on his fishing trouts at Zegwa)* and the frog Lady cane with the frog at low end and living person on the frog and living eagle at the top end. Then he make garment of glittering which her mother saw along side the Lake and supernatural Halibut, and a large Eagle that her mother saw in the midst sea while on her driven by the south-west wind. Then they give their mother new
                    the
chiefess names "Picking-Straw-Berries," and "Great-Haida-Woman." *(These names got it while they quarreling with that old chief wife a few days ago. So these people have this their name crest, and they*

had their mother moarning song while her escape from burning.)

And many years since that time their mother her children together, and she told them what happen to her.

Thus she said to them
Here is not our people, but our people away over on the other side of
this land, way out on the sea
and she told them
her story about
her brother Asdilthda on his way for
fishing trouts and how the frog
burned their city with fire, and how
she save alone, her father dugged
out the earth and put her into it with
many costly property and costly coppers six coppers, and so on, and
how she got the other village among
her relation with the same crest, and
how she driven by the south-west
wind, and so on till she had married
to your father.
Thus said the princess
to her children.

As soon as she end her story then one of the boys said, now let us go over and visit our native land and our relationship. Then the elder one has said let our young brother went forth and our young sister to visit them. So they are ready and went to their father. The Chief bought a new canoe that is good size on the sea or on the storms, and the mother went down on the beach.

Then she point
with her finger.
You must keep ahead between those Dundas
Island and Stephens Island, and when you went further out the sea
that you must keep ahead
where the sun set,
and you must keep the stern
at the sun rise,
and when you got over, along side that Island then turn your canoe on the south-west, then you shall find your grandfather's Village. Thus she said to her two children.

Then these children stard out with six slaves went along with these two young princes. They went farther on and on till they passed on between those two large Islands (Dundas and Stephens Island), they went further out the sea, as their mother command them. They ahead of their canoe at south-west, and after a little long, soon as the main land sink down, they saw the land before them, and they were glad. And on the next morning they landed on over the other shore and camp there a while. Again they stard along turn their canoe on the south, as their mother commanded them, and they went further on along side the island. As soon as they passed the first point they saw a Village before them, and before evening fall they arrived at the front of the Village. And young Princess spoke to it

     sirs if you lost a Princess

       while on her way to picking straw-berries

        since many years ago?

Then the people of the village called them ashore. And the people took them into the new chief house and they give out their story about their mother's driven away by the south-west her way for picking straw-berries, and some of them those that knew their mother was glad to hear a good news from the Princess that was lost long ago. Then the children told the people how his mother got a good new home among the Zimshean's tribe and how his elder brothers became rich and how many big feasting that was made, and his father was a chief in one of the Zimshean tribe. And at the end of his speech that his grantfather nephew invite all the chiefs and told them that his grantchildren come home safely, and they were all happy.

The boy went on the next day to visit his old first mother's home

     try to find the costly coppers and property

                that was hiding in

the earth

     as his mother told them.

               And he arrived at the old

desolate

     consumed

       village,

        Zegwa.

And he found all things

as his mother told them.

He found

all the costly copper and he found all the property.

And that the end.

Notes

1 "Zegwa": the Haida village of Djigua. Dalzell places it in the Cumshewa Inlet of Moresby Island and tells a version of the legend of the village's destruction by fire "under mysterious circumstances" (1973:263).

2 "Relation": clan. The hat is pictured on totem poles as tall and conical, having three or more cylinders surmounting the cormorant skin cap. It is one of several crests of the Eagle clan (or "relation"—Tate's word) that this story is designed to "copyright" for the teller's family.

3 "The Prince": Ashdilthda earns his name, which Tate translates as "Back-from-sea-to-shore." The compelling figure drawing the canoe repeatedly back to the shore is memorable.

4 "Her new parent": Deaksh is still on the Queen Charlottes. "The woman who survived fled around the coastline to Sandspit" (Dalzell 1973:264).

5 "Kitwilgeowatz tribe": Gitwilgyots, a Tsimshian village on the mouth of the Skeena River.

THE RAVEN CYCLE

Raven

There is no "complete" Raven cycle. Tate's thirty-seven stories, sent to Boas in two batches on 9 May 1905 and 7 February 1907, are a substantial number, but he acknowledged there were others he left out. Boas had asked specifically for the Raven myth and Tate was complying, but he held back because Raven does "very bad things" and "we are a live in the Christian life" (letter to Boas, 7 February 1907). Boas's response to Tate's hesitancy has become a celebrated model of anthropologist's grace in the face of danger:

> [I]f we want to preserve for future times a truthful
> picture of what the people were before they advanced to
> their present condition, we ought not to leave out any-
> thing that shows their ways of thinking, even though it
> should be quite distasteful to us (Letter 28 March 1907).

By that time, however, Tate had done as much as he was going to do with the Raven trickster stories.

Tate's disengagement is shown again in the fact that he sometimes took the short cut of using the published *Tsimshian Texts* (1902), the Nass River stories that Boas had sent to Port Simpson. Tate may very well have thought he had a specific directive to copy that source, in that Boas's letter of 23 June 1903 had asked him to write "in the manner of my Nass River book." The present selection generally avoids stories where Tate has been entirely dependent on the published versions.

Consequently, this necessarily limited sample is about one third of Tate's offered repertoire. It manages, however, to include a good many of the Raven classics that any audience would have a right to expect.

The History of Tkamshim

1. Origin of Raven

In his most elemental condition, Raven is a force which needs both human and bird form in order to complete the creation of the polymorphous perverse world as we know it. The initial entry of the supernatural into an incarnated being is imagined in a variety of ways in the corpus of northwest mythology (and Siberian as well). Tate's version is interesting for its Christ-like resurrection theme. It is said on good authority to be a Haida version (Henry Pierce to William Beynon, Columbia MS No.119). Much later, in 1954, Beynon elicited a very similar beginning from a Haida story-teller, Solomon Wilson of Skidegate (Barbeau 1961:83). Tate, however, in a letter to Boas of 6 July 1905, stated unequivocally that he was recording an authentic Tsimshian view as he had obtained it from three named fellow-residents of Port Simpson. In any case, Tate felt it necessary, in order to invoke a sense of the primeval, to set the initial action in a remote part of the Queen Charlotte Islands.

◆

There was once a land was covered with thick darkness, all over the world.

And there was a town of myth people at the south end of Queen-Charlotte-Island whose name is Kerouart Island.[1]

It was before human person was live.

There was a chief of myth people and chieftainess were living there which they had a son an only son their parents loved him most.

Therefore his father make a bed for his son above them, as a Prince sign of a great loving Prince to keep him away from danger.

So the boy father build his son's bed above them into his large house.

They washed him regularly, and he grow up to be a youth.

And when he was quite young, and soon he was got very sick.

Then the young man groaned for he was very sick, and not long enough that he was died.

Therefore his parents deeply sorrow and mourning over their loved one that was lost.

Then the chief sent and invite all his tribes.

At once all the myth people come in, and when they all entered the house of the chief, as soon as they were all in, then the chief said cut the belly of my dead son and take out the intestines.[2]

Therefore his attendants cut the belly of the chief's dead son and took out his intestines and they burned it behind the chief house.

And they place the corpse on his own bed which his father build for him.

The chief and chieftainess have their mourning song in every early morning under the corpse of his dead son, with his tribe come in and have lamentation with them.

They have done it day by day, as long as the young man was died.

Then on the next morning very early that the chieftainess got up first, and she look up to where her dead son layed.

Then she behold a bright young man was sating down to where the corspe was layed.

Therefore she woke her husband and she said to him,

Behold our loving son is alive again.

So the chief got up from his bed and he went at the foot of the long ladder that reached the top up to where the corpse was layed above them, and he ascending towards his son, and he (chief) said at once,

Is it you my loving son my pet is it you?

Therefore the bright young man had said yes it was I.

As soon as this bright young man says yes, then the chief and chieftainess has bursted into joy and gladness.

Then all his tribe came in as they did before to comfort their chief and chieftainess.

As soon as they entered they were much surprising for the bright young man was sat up now, and he spoke to them people,

The heaven was much annoyed for your often wailing every days, so he sent me down to comfort your sorrow.

So all the chief's tribe or his people was bursted into a great joy on that day, for their prince was alive again.

And the parents of this young man love him than they was love him before.

2. Raven becomes voracious

Tate is on track here with other versions. It seems to be held necessary that the ethereal nature of the other-worldly boy be desecrated, and the scavenger aspect of Raven come to the fore. Tate has the youth, prescient of his fate, bring about the voraciousness himself.

◆

Then this bright young man[3] ate not much food at this time.

Now he was there a long while, still he did not eat any food, but he was chewing just little of good fat so he don't eat any.

There the chief has two great slaves, one male slave and his wife, those slave was "Both-End-Mouth."

They went every morning and they brought all kinds of foods to the house of his master, and as soon as they came in from their hunts they cut out some large piece of whale's meats and cast them into the fire and ate them.

They has done it as often as they come home from hunting.

Then the chieftainess often try to give food to her resuscitated son, but he refused it he just lived by himself.

And the chieftainess was very anxious to let her son have some thing to eat.

She was afraid that her son will die again.

Then on the next day this bright young man take a walk to refresh himself, and as soon as he went out that the chief ascended up to a ladder where his thought his son bed above them.

Then behold the corpse of his own son layed there.

But he still glad to have his new son.

One day the chief and chieftainess went out for a while to visit their friends.

Then those two great slaves entered from their daily hunts as usually, which they brought in with them a large piece of whale's meat, their casted on the fire and immediately they ate.

Then the bright young man came toward them, and question those two great slaves,

What makes you so hungry?

Then those two great slaves replied because we have eat our own scabs from our shin.

So the bright young man said to them again, Is it sweet that you have eating now?

The male slave says, Yes, dear.

Then the prince say let me taste it and put your scab with the meat.

And the female slave says no my dear Prince, we don't want you to much eat as we are.

Again the young Prince have said, I'll just taste and I threw out of my mouth again.

So the male slave cutted a little piece of whale's meat with the smallest piece of his scab.

Then the female slave said with angry to her husband, Oh you naughty man, what have you been doing with my innocent Prince?

Then the bright Prince took up the little piece of meat with scabs or scale,[4] and put it into his mouth, to tasted.

He threw it again out of his mouth, and he went back up to his bed.

And soon the chief and chieftainess entered from their visiting.

Then the Prince say to his mother, I feel very hungry my mother.

The chieftainess said at once, Oh dear, it is sure, it is sure.

So she ordered her slaves to feed her loving son with richly food, so those slaves did.

They make ready with richly food of all kind of provisions, and the young Prince ate them all.

Again he was hungry, and the slaves feed him more than they feed him before.

He did so several days, and soon his father's house was empty with provisions.

Then the prince went round to every houses of his father's tribe and ate their provisions, because he tasted the scabs of "Both-End-Mouth."

Now the richly food was all used up.

The chief knew that his tribe's richly food almost all used up.

The great chief felt sad and ashame to what his son has done, for his son almost devoured the provisions of his tribe.

So he (chief) invites all the myth people and he said, I will sent my son away from me lest he devoured all your provisions and we will become wanting for food.

Then all the myth people agreed to which their chief has been said to them.

As soon as they were all agree, the chief called his son.

The the chief said that his son should stay in the middle of the rear of the house.

As soon as his son had sat down, then the chief had said to his son, My dear son I will send you away from me, towards Eastern country on the other side of the ocean.

He hand his son a small round stone, and Raven blanket, and dried sea-lion throat it filled all different kinds of wild fruits.

Then the chief had told his son, When you feel weary to flew away over this great ocean, then drop this round stone on the sea, then you shall find rest on it.

And then when thou hast got the main land, then you shall scatter these different fruits all over the land.

And you shall also scatter these salmon eggs into every river or creeks as well and trouts, so you shall not short for food as long as thou live on this our earth.

So he stard it

   Wi-Giat[5] his father named him

     and flew away

      toward the eastern country.

He went on for a long time, and finally he was very tired and wearied, so he dropped down little round stone on the sea which his father give it to him.

Then it became large rock, away out the sea.

And Wi-Giat have rested on it and refresh himself, and he took off the skin of the Raven, and have rested there for a while.

At that time it was always darkness, there was no day light.

Then Wi-Giat (or "Great-Person") he took the skin of Raven again and he put it on, and he flew again towards the East.

Now ("Great-Person") he reached into the main land, and arrived at the mouth of the Skeena River.

There he stood and scattered the salmon's and fishes' eggs.

He said during his scattered,

Let every Rivers and Creeks have all kinds of fishes.

And then he took a dried sea-lion throat, and scattered the fruits all over the land.

He said, Let every mountains, hills valleys plains or over the land filled with berries.

3. Raven steals daylight

Tate has already intimated that Wi-Giat will have to do something about the darkness. He has made "firmament" (at least an island—the mainland was already there) and he has, as Genesis puts it, "brought forth grass, and herb yielding seed," plus what is more important to the coastal Indians, he has stocked the rivers with salmon spawn. Now he must get to the problem of daylight, and he can't just say, "Let there be light." The general feeling is that Raven had to steal daylight from its myth owner. Immediately it is a test of his ingenuity, pushing him into his trickster role. As Minnie Johnson said to Frederica de Laguna, Raven had to "go through all that red tape to get it" (1972:842). And she adds, "It's a good deed he's doing though."

It still darkness was covered the whole world.

When the sky is clear and the myth people have a little light by the shines of many stars, and when the dark clouds was in the sky then it was thick darkness all over the land, and all the myth people was distressed at this reason.

Then Wi-Giat ("Great-Person") learned it's hard for himself to have his food if it was still dark.

So he remembered they have light enough in heaven to where he come from at first time.

Now he make up his mind and bring down the light to our world. On the next day he (Wi-Giat or "Great-Person") put on his Raven skin which his father myth chief give it to him, and flew upward.

Finally he has found the hole in the sky, and he flew through it.

When he reached the inside of the sky, "Great-Person" took off the skin of the Raven and he layed his skin of the Raven near the hole of the sky.

While "Great-Person" went on, he came to a spring near the chief of heaven's house.

There he sat down watching it.

He was waiting there little longer then the chief's daughter went forth and carrying a small basket in which she was about to fetch water.

She walked down to the spring in front of her father's house.

Then "Great-Person" show her coming along, he transformed himself into the leaf of a ceder, and floated on the water.

Then the chief's daughter dipped it up into her basket and drank it.

Then she returned to her father house.

She entered the house of her father.

After a short time she was conceived with child, and then not since that she gave birth to a boy.[6]

Then the chief and chieftainess were much glad.

They washed him regularly, the boy began to grow up.
Now he was beginning to creep about.

Then they washed him often, and the chief smoothed and cleaned the floor of his house.

Now the child was strong, and creeping around every day.

He began to cry all the time, Hama, hama.

Then the Great Chief was trouble and called some of his slaves to carry the boy around, so those slaves did, but he refused.

They never sleep in several night, his still crying Hama, hama.

So the chief invites all his wise men, and told them wise men he did not know what the boy wanted nor why he cried.

But he wanted the box that was hanging in the chief's house. This was a box in which daylight was kept hanging in one corner of his house. Its name was Mha.[7] Wi-Giat knows it before he was descended to our world. The child cried for it.

Then the chief was annoyed while those wise men heard the chief's conversational.

Then the wise men heard the child crying aloud.

They did not know what the child was saying, he cried all the time, Hama, hama, hama.

Now one of the wise men who understood him said to the chief, He is crying for the Mha.

So the chief ordered it to be taken down.

A man took it down.

They laid it down, and the boy sat down near it, ceased his crying.

He stopped crying, for he was glad.

Then he rolled it about inside the house.

He did so for four days.

Sometimes he carried it to the door.

Now the great Chief did not think of it, he was quite forgot it.

Then the boy really took the Mha.

He put it on his shoulders and ran out with it.

While he was running, someone said, "The Wi-Giat is running away with the Mha, ha."

Then he ran away with, then all the hosts of heaven pursued him.

They cried out that "Great-Person" ran away with Mha.

And he came to the hole of the sky.

Then he took the skin of the Raven, he put it on, and he flew down through the hole of the sky, Wi-Giat (or "Great-Person") carrying the Mhat.

Then all the hosts of heaven returned to their home.

He flew it down to our world.

At that time the world was still always dark.

He arrived farther up the river.

He walked down.

It was at the mouth of Naas river where Wi-Giat had come down.

Then Wi-Giat went on to the mouth of Naas river.

It was always dark, and he carried the Mhat about with him.

He went on and on up the river in the dark.

A little farther up he heard the noise of myth people who were catching Oolachen fishes in sack nets into their canoes.

There was a loud noise out on the river, because they were working hard.

130

The Wi-Giat, who was sitting on the shore, said, Throw ashore one of the things that you are catching, dear people.

Then Wi-Giat said again, Throw ashore one of the things you are catching.

Then they scolded him, those on the water, Where did you come from, you great liar?

It mean Tkamshim.[8] *The myth people knew that it was the Wi-Giat, therefore they made fun of him.*

Then "Great-Person" said again, Throw ashore one of the thing you are catching, or I shall break the Mha.

And all of them that was on the water answered, Oh where did you get what you are talking about, you great liar?

Wi-Giat said once more, Throw ashore one of the things you are catching, dear people, or I shall break to you the Mha.

And a person replied to him badly.

The Wi-Giat repeated his request four times but those on the water refused what he asked for.

Therefore "Great-Person" broke the Mha.

It broke, and it was daylight.

And then the north winds blew hard with the daylight, harder and harder.

Then all them fishing men, frogs drivened away by the north winds.

Then all them frogs who made fun with Wi-Giat drivened away down until they arrived on one of the large Island mountain.

Here is all the frogs trying to climb up the rock, yet they sticked to the rock by the frozen of north winds.

There are now on the rock.[9] *They became to a rock. Those fishers frogs name him Tkamshim.*

Now the world have daylight.

4. Stone and Elderberry bush

This little fable was often told without Raven entering into it. But mortality is something of a dirty trick, and Tate is emphatic that Raven was the operative factor: "The people are not live before Tkamshim coming down of our earth, until Tkamshim made person out of elderberrie tree" (letter to Boas 6 July 1905).

◆

Then Tkamshim went along up to Naas.

He came to where the Stone and Elderberry Bush quarreled among themselves to whom shall be gave birth first.

The Stone wished to gave birth first, and Elderberry Bush wished to gave birth first.

And Tkamshim listen to what they say.

The Stone had said if I gave birth first the the person live longer or else if you give birth first then the people's lives were short.

So Wi-Giat went near where they were and he look and behold the Stone she almost her delivered, and he went toward the Elderberry Bush and he touched her.

He said give birth first Elderberry Bush.

Then the Elderberry Bush give her birth.

For that reason the people do not live many years. It's because the Elderberry Bush gave birth to her children first men dies quickly. Or if the Stone had first given birth to her children, this would not be so.[10] Thus our people say. That is the story of the Elderberry Bush's children. So the Indians are much troubled because the Stone did not give birth to her children first. For this reason the people dies soon. And the Elderberry Bush grow on their grave.

5. Raven (Deer) steals fire

Raven is not really needed in this fable, which aims to explain the short black tail of the deer. The story often appears without him (Boas 1916:660), but Tate wants Raven to be a creative culture hero as well as a trickster, and has him be Deer in disguise.

Again went on, and the people began to multiply on the face of the earth.

They had distressed for they have no fire to cook their food and to warmed in winters.

And Wi-Giat remembered they had a fire enough in his myth people Chief Village.

So he went and try to bring over to the people.

He went over, he worned his blanket of Raven which his father the chief of myth people gave it to him before he left him yonder.

He soon arrived there, but the myth people of the Village which his father tribe refused to let him have a fire from them, and they sent him away from their country.

He was tried every way to get fire, but he was failed, for those myth people would not to let him have.

Finally he has sent one of his attendant, this Seagull, and bring message to those myth people, and this is the message that the seagull brought.

A good young chief shall come in sometime with all his myth people to have a good dances in your chief house.

Then all the chief's tribe ready to welcome the young chief.

Then Wi-Giat caught the Deer and skinned it.

They went to those Village.

(At that time the Deer has a long tail as like as a Wolf's tail.)

Wi-Giat bind firebrand on the long tail of a Deer.

He loaned to a canoe of White-shark.

They came to a Village of myth people to where the chief had a large fire in his house.

All the Crows and Seagulls full in a large White-shark canoe, and Wi-Giat in the center of the canoe with his Deer skin on.

Then all the crowds of myth people entered.

They build a large fire than it was before.

The large house of the chief's was full up with his tribe. Then all those new cometh seated on one side of a large house, ready to sing.

Soon the young chief began to dance.

Then all his companion beat their stick, and one had a drum. Then they all sang a song and some of the birds clapped their hands with a loud, sang a song.

And this is their song.[11]

Then the Deer came in at the door.

He look round and entered leaping and dancing, went around a large fire.

Then all the myth people well very pleased to see him dancing around.

Finally he strucked his tail over the fire.

Then the firebrand on his tail burned.

He ran out with firebrand at his tail and he swimmed on the water.

Therefore all his companion flew away, out from the house.

Their White-shark canoe went away also.

They tried to catch him, intending to kill him.

He jump, and swim quickly and the firebrand at his tail burned.

Then he arrived on one of the Island, he went ashore quickly and strucked every trees on that Island with his tail.

And he said, You shall ever burned as long as the years was.

So that reason the Deer have a short tail with black.

He took again his Raven blanket and flew again over the ocean with the firebrand in his hands.

He arrived at main land.

6. Raven and the Tide-woman

It is an old woman, like one of the prior generation of Titans, who controls the tides. Where did she come from? We are not told in any of the versions. She is the given. But her age does not stop her being offered indignities by Raven, who must have the cockles that she hides with her high tides.

◆

He went on.

Wi-Giat found another house which belong to a very old woman which kept and held the tide-line in her hand.

At that time it was the tide always high, it cannot be turn for several days until the new moon, and all the people anxious for clams and so on.

Now Wi-Giat went into and found an old woman was hold the tide-line in her hand.

He sat down and he said, Oh I am well filled satisfied, I got all the clams I needed.

At once the old woman has said, how can it be? where does that come from that you are speaking of Wi-Giat?

Yes, I am full with fresh clams.

The old woman had to say, No you won'd.

Therefore Wi-Giat rushed her backward and put powder sand into her eyes, also into her mouth.

Then she let her tide-line go.[12]

So the tide ran down, very low, and all them clams and them shell-fishes aground.

So Wi-Giat carried them up as much as he can.

The tide is still low, he went in again.

And old woman have said, Wi-Giat come and heal my eyes, for I am blind with sand.

And Wi-Giat ask her, Will you give me an oath? I want you to slack down your tide-line twice a day.

Therefore she was agreed, and Wi-Giat cured her eyes.
He has ate all them shell-fishes that he carried up.

Soon after he ates, therefore the old woman said, How can you have water to drank, Wi-Giat?

The answered was, Under the root of little Alder tree.[13]

Soon Wi-Giat has thirsting, he went for water to drink, but he cannot find.

He went farther on, he found none.

Finally he went up to Skeena, there he found water, because the old woman dried all the brooks and creeks.

And so the tide turned often every day, up and down.

7. Raven and the Bullhead

Tate has a source for this short "just-so" story in *Tsimshian Texts* (1902), Boas's Nass River texts. Boas had sent this publication to Port Simpson as a model, and Tate used it as such, especially for the Raven series, sometimes following it quite closely, as here (1902:37-38). What is interesting, in terms of Tate as a creative writer, is to see what he adds: In this story, it is the coaxing of the Bullhead by saying that he looks like a dear departed grandfather—a nice touch.

◆

He went along the side of the sandbar point.

And while he was walking along, he went toward the beach searching for some food, but he did not find anything.

At once, he behold there was a fish in the water.

It was not moving.

Then Tkamshim stood there.

He was wept.

He said to the fish, You looks like my grantfather that was died little while ago.

He wiped off his tears from his eyes,

He said, Come here ashore, or I will talk to you a while. The fish came toward the shore.

Tkamshim thought he would kill it.

Then Tkamshim was much depressed because he was hungry. Now it was almost within reach, but it swam back into the water.

The fish knew his intentions.

It swam back from the shore saying, What, do you think I do not know you, Wi-Giat?

Then he acted as though he were taking hold of the image of the fish, and stretched out his hand, and said,

You shall have a thin tail. Only your head shall be large or thick.

Then it became the Bullhead.

So the Bullhead used to be remarkably stout. For Tkamshim cursed it, and therefore it is thin at one end and the other end was thick.

8. Raven pretends to be a shaman

Why does Raven pretend to be a shaman? To cure the princess? If you can believe that, you can believe anything. As Boas says, this story "is very much toned down" (1916:722). The way it should be told is too coarse for Tate to offer. Readers must imagine for themselves what Raven is really doing under the cedar-bark mat.

◆

Then he went on not knowing which way to turn.

He was very hungry.

He was alone in a lonely place, and soon he found the end of the large town.

He saw many people walking up and down.

Then he was afraid to let them people see him.

Now Tkamshim sat there.

And on the next day, while he sat there still, he behold a large canoe launched out from that Village loaded with many young women went for picking blue berries yonder.

Tkamshim make up his mind how to get in that great town yonder.

Finally he thought to caught a deer.

So he went up into the wood, and caught a deer, and skinned it.

He put its skin on, and he swammed before the large canoe that loaded with many young women went to picking blue berries.

Then one young princess, a daughter of the head chief of that large town that Tkamshim saw away yonder, was among these young women.

She sat down near the middle of a large canoe between two young women.

Now they saw a male deer swammed along before their canoe.

So the young princess say to her companion, Let us pursue him.

So they did.

They paddle away, and soon they caught him and kill him, and they have him in their canoe.

Tkamshim spue and said in his heart, Let them lay me at the front of a young princess.

Then they took him in the canoe and layed him at the front of a young princess, as Tkamshim spue them.

Then they paddle along toward blue berries were.

Then before they reach on the ground where the blue berries were, the deer moved his hind leg.

Then he kicked the young princess by her belly.

He leaped out from the canoe, and he went in the woods again.

Now the young princess fainted on account of her hurt. So these young women turned and went home, the princess worse more and more, until they reach at the beach of the head chief's house.

They told the people what happened to them along their way.

Then they took the young princess up to her father's house followed with a great number of people.

Then the chief sorrow was very much on the cause of his only daughter get hurt.

Then he called together all his wise men, and ask them which is the best thing to do to heal his daughter.

Then his wise men said that he should gather all the sorcerers, and try to cure her hurt.

(Her under ribs has a hole hurt by the hind leg of a deer.)

Then Chief order his attendants to invite all the magicians.

So his attendants went and invite all the sorcerers.

Then all the sorcerers gather together in great into the house of the chief.

Then the magicians worked on with their enchantments, but they all failed, the hurt could not cure by the enchantments of the sorcerers.

Then the girl more worse and worse, till she was very ill.

But still the sorcerers worked on day and night.

Then when three days passed on while those many sorcerers worked in vain, and on the fourth day, behold a large canoe filled with young men came into the town.

At before the evening fall, she reach ashore, then some people went down.

Then those men coming down saw a Sorcerer sat in the middle of a large canoe.

Then they went up quickly and they told to the chief that a sorcerer came into a town.

So the chief sent for him to cure his only daughter.

(That's Tkamshim this sorcerer, his grantchildren crows was his crews in his canoe.)

Then he came in at the evening, he saw the young princess lay there very ill, for he hurt her few days ago.

Then all those sorcerers that was failed before sat back on one side of the house.

Tkamshim was pretended to a Sorcerer.

He sat down at the head of a princess lay.

Then all his young people followed in with a large box of his enchantments.

He took the charcoals and rubbed it on his face and also rubbed the ashes over it.

He put on the claws-bear crown, placed a ring of red ceder bark around his neck.

Also he put on his Sorcerer dance apron, took up his large Sorcerer rattle.

He started just drum and beating, and this is the latter sang, after drum and beating, then while they sang, they pronounce the words, is this.

> Let the mighty hail fell
> on this chief house roof
> on the chief house roof
> on the chief house roof.

And as the singer pronounce these words that the mighty Hail beated on the roof of the chief's house very fearful.

(Before Tkamshim arrived at the town, he order some of his grantchildren crows that each one of them should have on their mouth a little piece of white stone. When we pronounce the words or our song, then you shall drop them on the chief house roof, thus said Tkamshim to his grantchildren crows. So they did.)[14]

And while a mighty hail was ceased, Tkamshim ask and said, Bring up to me a cedar-bark mat.

Then they brought to him mat.

He took it and spread it over the princess to cover her.

He went also under it with the girl.

He touch the wound and had said, Cure on under right ribs.

So it was.

Then the Chief was very glad for his daughter was healed from her hurt.

Then he fed Tkamshim of all kinds of food.

Now the Chief ask the Sorcerer, after he fed him, he said, Ask of me whatsoever thou wilt, and I will give it to you.

He sware unto him, Whatsoever thou shalt ask of me I will give it to you, my dear, good and true familiar spirit, you had an enchantments, for you are able to restored my only daughter to well again.

Then Tkamshim look around and smile.

What I want is you should move and leave to me all the provision you had, for my young men have none, for we had no time to earn ours, for we went round often times to healing those who need us.

Then the Chief order his slave, Go out and order the people to move tomorrow.

The slave ran out crying, Move great tribe, and leave of your provision behind.

The people did so, they moved in the morning, they left all their food by the order of their head chief.

Tkamshim was very glad because he has much food at this time.

Then on the next day he take a walk, and while he was absent his grantchildren were gather together and they opened many boxes of crab-apple that mixed with grease.

They ate them all.

When Tkamshim came home from his walking, behold all the empty boxes he saw.

He knew that his grantchildren has done that.

That is the end of another adventure of Tkamshim.

9. Raven in the house of Echo

This is entirely a dream. You come upon a house where food appears of its own accord, echoing your wishful thinking. But you always want more than you are given. You reach for the forbidden, and wake up with a punishing blow to your ankles. You limp away, hungry still.

◆

Tkamshim sit down there quietly thinking how many difficulties that he has done among the human people, yet he was not satisfied for what he need.

At last he make up his mind to tried to go again among the myth people to get something to eat, for he was a great eater.

Then so he went into the desert place and his very anxious to find some myth people in the woods.

Soon he arrive to a great plain, no trees to be seen, just grass and flowers and a far distance there he beheld a large house.

And he heard many people singing inside the large carving-front house.

And he saw a sparks flew up from the smoke hole of the large house, and he knew a great chief's house was there.

Then when he came near towards the house, he heard some one have said with a loud voice,

Some strange came along towards us. The chief is coming.

And he knew they mean him.

So he went in and he saw no man, but the voices he heard.

Then he saw a large fire in the centre, and a good new mat being spread for him along the side of the fire.

Then he heard a voice which call him on the mat which said with loud voices, This way great chief, this way great chief, this way.

He walked in proudly towards the mat.

Then Tkamshim sat down on it.

(This house is the house of a chief Echo.)

Then Tkamshim heard a chief saying to his slaves that they might roast a dry slamon.

Then he behold a carving box opened of itself, and dried salmon came out of it.

Again he saw a good dish walk towards the fire all itself.

Tkamshim was much afraid and astonished to see these things.

Now when the dry salmon already roasted and cut it right length, they all went into the dish.

It lay down in the front of Tkamshim.

He thought it about while he was eating how strange thing he saw.

Now, when he finished, a dipper of horn came forward full with water in it.

He took it by its handle then he drank.

Then he saw a large dish was full with cab-apples mixt with grease.

And black horn spoon came forward by itself, Tkamshim took the handle.

Then he ate all he could.

Then before he empty his dish he look around, behold a large mountain goat's fat was all hunging on one side of the house, and he thought,

I will took down one of those large piece of fat there. Thus Tkamshim thought while he was eating.

Then he heard a many womens laughing on one corner of the house,

Ha! ha! I will took down one of those large mountain goat's fat, thus Tkamshim thought it now.

Then Tkamshim was ashame for what womens have to said.

And soon he ate all crab-apples.

Again another dish came forward full with cranberries mixt with grease and with water.

Tkamshim was ate again.

He behold a dried goat meat was hunging there on one corner of the large house.

He thought once more, I shall took down one of those mountain sheep goat meat there, and I will run out.

Again he heard many womens laught once more,

Ha! ha! I shall took down one of those mountain sheep goat meat there and I will ran out with, that's Tkamshim thought just now.

Now Tkamshim was trouble for what those women he heard them laught at one corner of the house.

Then he got up and ran out and snatch one of a large mountain goat meat and also a large fat.

But when he came to the door that a large stone hammer beat him by his ankle-bone.

Soon he fell down on the ground, with a badly hurt, and lose those meat and fat.

And some one dragged him out, and cast him out.

He lay there a long while with his ankle-bone quite very sore.

He began to cry, for he was very hungry and his foot very sore.

And on the next day, that he got little better, he got his stick and tried to walk away.

10. Raven and Little Pitch

This gem of a story shows the consummate psychopathic con artist at work, with a victim as agreeable as any one of us unwary folk might be. Raven, this time, doesn't get anything at all for his efforts. In fact, it seems a fantasy: what a jail-bird dreams of doing when he gets out of clink. But Raven is imprisoned in his own nature for life.

So he went on, not knowing which way to go.

He was very weak and very hungry, and sore foot.

He went on and on in the woods until he saw a house afar off, and went towards it, came nearer and nearer, he went in.

A man and his wife, a very fair young woman, they permitted him to come in, for they had compassion on this poor man came up to their house.

They ask him if he want to have some thing to eat, and they gave him to eat.

Then the fair young woman try to cure his ankle-bone that was hurt with stone in the house of the chief Echo.

The house of Little Pitch he got in now.

And these people so very kind to him, the wife of Little Pitch put pitch on his sore ankle-bone.

Two days after, he got a perfectly cure, he was glad now, the young woman give him well feed every day, the house of Little Pitch fill with dry halibut and all kinds of provisions.

Tkamshim made of his mind to kill his kind friend which kindly intreat.

On the next evening after he ate his supper, he said to his friend that they would go to catch halibut tomorrow morning.

Little Pitch is willing, and he said to Tkamshim,

It is not good for me if I out fishing in the sunshine I am so weak.

I must return home while it is still chilly.

And Tkamshim said, Whatever you said sir I will do it. I think we shall have enough time, Tkamshim replied.

Then they starded on their fishing grown.

They fishing all night, until the day-break, and when the sun rose up Little Pitch wanted to go home.

But Tkamshim said, I enjoy the fishing, lie down there, in the bow of the canoe, and cover yourself with a mat.

Little Pitch lie down.

Then Tkamshim called him, Little Pitch?

Hi, he replied.

After a while Tkamshim called him again, Little Pitch?

Hi, he answered again with a loud voice.

Again Tkamshim called him, Little Pitch?

Hi, was he answered with a little low voice.

Tkamshim called him again.

Hi, he answered with a very weak voice.

Now I'll pull up my fishing line.

And when he hauled his line all into the canoe that he paddle away towards home.

Tkamshim strong paddled away.[15]

He called again, Little Pitch?

No answered came.

So he went to see what happened to Little Pitch, and soon as he touch the mat that cover Little Pitch, behold the pitch ran out over all the halibut.

He died there and melted all over the halibut. Therefore the halibut is black on their back or on one side.

Tkamshim was glad.

He paddled alone until he reached on the shore at the front of Little Pitch house, expecting to have a good supper from Little Pitch wife, and took the line to tied his canoe, went up gladly, and went on and on, but cannot find a house.

He searched everywhere, but he could not find but only little green spruce tree stood with a drop of pitch on one side.

Finally Tkamshim remember his canoe was full with halibut, so he went down on the beach with hungry.

He could not found his canoe, but a spruce log was there with her roots.

11. Raven imitates Seal

This is one of the very popular "bungling host" stories, exemplifying a universal trait: the conspicuous effort to compete in hospitality (Boas 1916:694; Thompson 1929:1). In itself a benign enough ambition, it becomes ludicrous when you assume what worked for your host will work for you. Raven as host seems almost out of character; but he makes a mess of it, so that's all right.

◆

He went again.

When he reached to a long point, behold a house was there.

He went in, for he was very hungry.

(This is the house of Seal.)

The chief Seal spread a new mat and Tkamshim sat on it.

First thing the seal roast a dry salmon put in a dish and place it before Tkamshim.

The Seal took another dish and placed it near the fire.
Then he held both hands near the fire on the back of his hands so that they grew warm.

The grease dripped from his fingers and ran into the dish.

He gave it to Tkamshim to dip his salmon, and Tkamshim dip his salmon in the grease, and he ate.

Next took a dish and fill it with the seal blubbers and put more grease over it.

Tkamshim was very glad, he was satisfy in the house of Seal.

Then he left

Now he build a house.

He finish it.

Now he invited the Seal to his new house.

Then the Seal came to visited and he sat him at rear of his house.

Tkamshim took a dish, he placed it near the fire, and he held up his hands so that grew warm, and his fingers' eyes and mouth was scorched.

They the olden people said that all the joint of man's or women's fingers have eyes and mouths. Since Tkamshim held up his hands while invited the chief Seal into his house that the man's fingers have no eyes and no mouth. While the person ate food in those days, fingers also ate food. [16]

Tkamshim fell back as dead man.

He lie there all while.

Then the Seal rose.

There was no grease in the dish.

He said, He tries to do what I do.

Tkamshim was very much ashame.

He rose up went in the woods and found pitch and put it on his fingers.

12. Raven turns the monsters into rocks

This story, the last of the Raven cycle in Tate's manuscript, has Raven ending as a rock. There is a hint of self-sacrifice here, as though, in turning all the monsters into stone, Raven knew he must suffer the same fate himself.

◆

Now Tkamshim has been away from this country quite a long while, many many years his been away.

And when he come back from there, Alaska, with his old Raven garment on, he made a great feast to all kinds monstrosity at one of the outer Island.

Now when all them guests was enter at the Bay on one side of that Island, Tkamshim was forth to see his guests was full on the water at the front of Tkamshim new-build carving house.

This feast was first stard from Tkamshim, it was potlatch, and invites all different kinds of monstrosities.

When they come into the Bay, Tkamshim came forth from his house, he stood outside of his door, and he began to talked to all his guests.

Now my dear all the chiefs, I am so very glad to see that you all come into my Potlatch. Though I been away from this country a long time, so I was glad to see you again at this time. Now one thing I want to say more beside this. You might remain there and you became all stones.

Then all those different kinds of monstrosity became stones.

And I will also became of stones.

As soon as Tkamshim have said, then the Devilfish sink down quickly when Tkamshim mention they will became a stones.

So the Devilfish remain at the bottom of the sea now.

Then all them monstrosities became stones.

It very please to the people to see them now.

And also Tkamshim himself became a stone as like Raven.

But only Devilfish alive now.

So when the people say now-a-day before monster of Devilfish come out on the water then the people used Raven cried caw! caw! caw!

*Then the large Devilfish died when she heard the Raven caw!
caw! caw!* [17]

*That Island was full with stones shape of all kinds of monsters,
Whales, large Grampus, Sharks, and so on.*

And the Raven stood at the front of his carving house now. [18]

This is the special end.

Notes

1 "Kerouart Island": Kerouard Islands, adjacent to Cape St. James, the
southernmost point of the Queen Charlotte Islands (Dalzell 1973:150).
Only "myth people" or sea-lions could inhabit those rocks. Solomon
Wilson thought the origin of Raven might be there or the nearby Ninsints
village, the historic site of St. Anthony Island (Barbeau 1961:83). It should,
however, be pointed out that Tate's Tsimshian line gives the place-name
as Kungalashs, which, as Boas surmised (1916:58), would be the old village of Kunhalas, at Cumshewa Head, a much more civilized setting.

2 "Intestines": Tate elsewhere told Boas that this was an actual practice
of the Tsimshian.

> In olden times it was the custom that when a prince or
> rich man, or a chieftainess or princess, or somebody who
> was dear to them, died, they cut the corpse and took out
> the bowels, stomach, heart, liver, and lungs; and when
> the body was empty, they put shredded red-cedar bark
> into it, and they kept the body for a long while
> (1916:337).

We should also note the belief that "the Raven has no intestines"
(1916:96), which may have been in Tate's mind when he composed this
first segment of the story.

3 "Bright young man": The Tsimshian word for "prince,"
Lthguwalkshuk in Tate's spelling, is the title "applied to the sons of a
chief, who are as young and promising of wealth and plenty as the young
salmon on its way down the river to the sea" (Halpin 1973:148). Inherent
in the etymology of the word is "bright and silvery young salmon." Thus,
the young man's halo may be due less to a quasi-Christian sanctity than to
the sheen of salmon skin.

4 "Scabs or scale": This minute amount of what could be called "dead
flesh" must be connected in some way to the frenzied hunger of the initiates to the Cannibal societies. Tate described these rituals to Boas
(1916:546-49), but did not make this specific connection with Raven.

147

5 "Wi-Giat": Tate translates this name literally as "Great-Person." A recent collection of Tsimshian stories by the Book Builders of 'Ksan is entitled *We-gyet Wanders On* (Saanichton, B.C.: Hancock House, 1977); a footnote to the preface states: "We-gyet rhymes with 'be set.' In English We-gyet means 'big man'."

6 "Birth to a boy": The parallel with the virgin birth of the New Testament did not escape some of Frederica de Laguna's informants (de Laguna 1972:843), though one of them also added a more mundane thought: "That's why people on earth have so many fatherless kids. Raven is the one to get that started."

7 "Mha": apparently an untranslatable proper name. Boas glosses it merely as "receptacle in which the sun was kept" (1916:971).

8 "Tkamshim": Tate seems to indicate that Raven's name means "liar." There is no confirmation of this meaning elsewhere.

9 "Rock": no specific location for this rock is given. Other versions have the fishing people metamorphosed into a variety of land and sea creatures. There is some reason to suppose that the original idea of the story was that these were ghost creatures who would have to flee with the light, but that meaning has entirely dropped out.

10 "Not be so": "Only fingernails and toenails show how the skin would have been if stone's children had been born first" (Boas's *Indianische Sagen* version, quoted and discussed by Cove 1987:52).

11 "Song": no doubt Tate meant to add words and music later, but he didn't.

12 "Let her tide-line go": One wonders if Tate has not cleaned up his version somewhat. In a Tlingit narrative Raven beats the tide-woman's behind with sea-urchins until she says, "That's enough, Raven! That's enough, Raven!"—which phrase has become the way boys say "enough" in a fight (de Laguna 1972:845). The tides keep moving today because the old woman still can't sit still (de Laguna 1972:859).

13 "Alder tree": This has a significance which is not explained. The same phrase occurs again in the Raven stories (1916:69), where Raven expects to find water at the root of the alder tree, but it has dried up.

14 "So they did": Tate confirms our general suspicion that shamans must have used assistants to help them create supernatural effects. It is difficult to find evidence in the ethnological data.

15 "Strong paddles away": The *Tsimshian Texts* (1902) version, which Tate was paraphrasing, makes sure we understand that Raven is in no hurry to get to shore:"He pretended to paddle strongly, but he put his paddles into the water edgewise" (Boas 1902:59-60). Tate missed this out. Perhaps he would expect us to know it.

16 "Fingers also ate food": Tate adds this bit of lore to the story as he found it in Boas (1902:46-47).

17 "Caw!": Tate expands on this belief in a story "The Giant Devilfish," for which we have no manuscript. The pertinent passage was transcribed by Boas as follows:

> When the people in olden times saw a devilfish coming up under a canoe, sometimes a man would sing out like a raven, "Caw, caw, caw!" Then the great monster would die before it came to the surface of the water. The devilfish would always die when it heard the sound of the raven's voice; but if a person waited until the monster came to the surface of the water and then sang out, it was in vain, and the great monster would swallow him, canoe and all (1916:138).

18 "Now": Tate does not reveal the location of the "outer island" where these monster rocks and raven image can be seen. A totem pole called "Whereon-sleeps-the-Raven" stood close to the beach at Port Simpson in Tate's time (Barbeau 1950:348).

Raven is Alive

In the late summer of 1907, just back from the "fishing ground at the Skeena," Tate sent off "the last part of Tkamshim" (letter to Boas, 29 August 1907). He had been talking to his cousin Henry Pierce, who told him about somebody he had met who had seen Tkamshim alive. Tate got the whole story. There are a few folkloric themes in this piece, but the form is that of a personal anecdote told by the participant, a young man who tells of coming upon Tkamshim's present-day house. Tkamshim has shed his Raven form, and is a sort of a Sasquatch.

The further history of Tkamshim

Now there was a great chief of the Gilauzui tribe, named Dhamnunk. At three years since the white men reached this country and before this great chief Dhamnunk made a great feasts to all the Zimshean tribes that he build a house, a very good carving house, carving at the front outside and carving also at the interior. All the lumbers at the interior was goodly carving than the outer carvened. And when he finished he invites all them Zimshean chiefs to his new carvening house. And when all them chiefs come in they are very delight to see those beautiful carvened at the interior of Dhamnunk's house on that day. And all them Zimshean nation spread the fame of Dhamnunk's house, how nice it is, and all the people round about the Zimshean nation talked how good Dhamnunk carvening house. So all them people round about came to show and see that house. Finally all them animals also heard the fame of Dbamnunk's house was very nice.

Now Tkamshim heard also these thing.

Every day since Chief Dhamnunk finish his house the people always fill his house with the people, and every night all kinds of animals came in to see the interior carvened. This goodly house he build at Skeena River at the mouth of Klakgilish River, that the village of Gilauzui tribe.[1]

Now at the latter on it before Spring, while the people ready for Naas fishing Oolachen, and at midnight the chief Dhamnunk was sleepless with his wife and he behold his door was secretly opened and he awoked his wife. What is the matter? They look, and they behold door a great man was enter there. He was creeping when he got in and he began to shown the interior carvened. And before that giant finish his show, then the chief fill with fear. So he was groan on account of fear. Therefore the giant went forth quickly.

And on the following morning the Chief invite all his own people and showed them what happen to his house on the night past. So all his men agreed to watch on the next night. And when the night came on, three men lay wait at the door. One of the chief's men has a gun he loaded with five bullets. And before midnight that the door was secretly opened again as it was before. Behold a great man came creeping in, and saw the carvening that he was not finish last night. Therefore those three men that lay in wait ready shot him. And the man that had the gun first was faint, so the other have courageous and took the gun from the other and shot him on his breast with the five bullets. But the giant took no notice of it. And all them men that lay in wait all was fainted. The Chief no faint it at all. When the giant got the show through, when he finish every lumber's carvening, then went forth.

150

And these men don't know who it was that they shot.

Now at the end of these time these people was afraid if they shot the supernatural.

And many years past on. Two years since cannery were working at the Skeena River not many years ago,[2] the young man up the upper Skeena has a gamble with his fellow man, and lost all his goods, nothing was left to him, and also his wife and his two children. Therefore he was wroth with grief, for his wife has nothing to wear, no clothes and no food to her children. So this young man went away from his bare empty lonely home. He wandering away far among the mountain, many mountain he has past over it. And when he past over many mountains and came at the border of a great plain, then he got in a very small trail. He went on and on, finally he behold a smoke ascented at distance. Therefore he went towards it, and when he reached there and found a great pit, and he stood at the brim of a great pit, and he look down, then he saw a hut was in the pit, and the smoke ascented from it. He look another way, then he see the same trail that he had in afar went straight down at the front of that little hut. So he went down by that trail.

He look secretly in the hole, and great man lay there with his back against the fire. He said to a young came secretly at his door,

Come in, sir, for I know you ever since you wandering away from you Come in my dear man.

So the young man came in.

The giant set up, and he look at the young man. He began to say and put his question to the young man,

Did you know the natives' history about Tkamshim?

The young answered, Yes.

Then the giant (Tkamshim) continue, I am he, says he. You see this breast was wound? I received these in the carvening house of Dhamnunk.

But this young man wonderful at him. This young man not know the carvening house of Dhamnunk.

This giant was Tkamshim.

Then he said to this young man, I will give you meat.

So he did. And after the young man had his dinner Tkamshim had said, The almighty give me this valley to live, and he fed me.

As soon as the young man came into the hut, he saw two little pups lied at the side of the fire. And Tkamshim called forth the young man. When they went out both Tkamshim pointed with his finger all round the mountains stood all round his hut, and all them mountains were full with mountain sheeps, some mountains full with black bears, with all kind of animals. Tkamshim had said moreover,

You see all those animals? They are all my provisions the almighty prepared for me. The almighty command me that I will stay here a little longer. So I did not went round over the world any more. But I shall go round once more in the future day I don't know, but the almighty himself his only to know.

After he speak, he called them little pups by their names. Then those pups rosed up and they shaked their bodies and they became two young Lions.[3] Therefore the young man afraid, but Tkamshim sent those two young Lions on one of the mountain that was full with mountain sheeps. So they did. Then Tkanshim told the young man, The almighty give me those two young Lions to bring my meat every days. And while Tkamshim had said these words they heard the growling of two young Lions that went on the mountain. Behold a great number of mountain goats fell from the mountain at one side of Tkamshim hut. Then Tkamshim skinned them and cut them all. When he finished cutting took of meats and fattings, then he took one hunting cane and wrapped all them fats on his cane. When the cane was thick with fats, Tkamshim squeeze. He wrap some more. He done it four times. Then all the fats finished. Then he also took meats and wrapped them again over on the top of fats on over the same cane. When it thick he squeezed, and the cane was thin again. He done it four times. Then all the meats was finished, and Tkamshim hand it to the young man.

He said to him, You go back home.

Then the young man had said, I did not know my way, for it's very long way off. I don't think I will not arrive at my home.

Therefore Tkamshim led him up on one of the hill and point him.

Further you shall go where I point. You can go by that small trail yonder. This trail reached behind your home. You soon got home.

Then the young man said, I been traveler for many days. How can get home soon?

Tkamshim said, I will smooth your way. You shall reach home tonight. Keep your eyes on the small trail. Or if you heard any thing behind you on the way, like as thunder or terror noise, don't look back, lest some perils come to you on the way. Keep your eyes on the trail until thou reach above your village safely, then you shall look back, and you shall know what happened.

Then Tkamshim had said, Have patience young man, look not behind thee.

Then the young man made swear by oath that he will not look behind on his way down to his home.

Now he was ready. Tkamshim told him, Try to go quickly as you could. The man took his own rifle on his left shoulder and Tkamshim's cane held on his right hand. Then Tkamshim said, Go on quick, my dogs will soon come and devour you. Therefore the young man went, and keep his eyes on the small trail. The trail went in the middle of a large plain. When he ran, then he heard a great noise like as thunder rolling. But the young man keep on going. Some more terrors he heard right close behind him, as the noise of the mountain falls, and the earth trembled on his way. But he keep his eyes on the small trail. More terrible noise he heard behind him, and he run with all his might, try to escape from the terrors that close behind him. And more trembled of the ground he went and soon he fear, but he was keep ahead. And before the sun set he arrived above his village

and stood there.

Then he look back.

He behold the tops of all mountains appears to where he came. Tkamshim smooths all them mountains before this young man went, and as soon as this man past on one mountains then that same mountain stood up as it was before, so it makes a terrible noise. For all them mountains stood up again in their own place, no large plain and no small trail to be seen, only the top mountains covered behind this man.

He wonderer for what happen to him. He stood there a while. He thought that he was dreamt. He still held the cane on his right hand and his own rifle on his left shoulder. And he made of his mind to go down the village, and he layed down his cane and his rifle. He leaned his cane on the stump.

So he went down to his father's house, and he look in secret in the hole, and he beheld his sister wept on the side of a fire, and many people around the fire looks so very sorry. So he went in secretly. He went towards his sister that was weeping. He sat at his sister's side and talk to her.

My sister, said he, did my wife live now?

And his sister was astonished to see him.

So all the people gladly to see him home again. His poor wife came in with his two children. The man took up his two children on his knees. He ordered his nephews to invite all his tribes.

So they did as their uncle said. Then when all the guests came in that the man went up to where his cane layed with his four nephews, and these four young men cannot lift up that cane. So the man took down by himself to his house, and placed it at the front interior of the house. And he ordered to spreads their mats at the part of his father's house, and the man loose the meats of mountain sheeps. It pile them a great heap. Also he loose all the fats on cane. He heaps fats by itself. And when he empty his cane, then he given his part of meats to his people, and some fats.

And he told them his story.

> As I went wanderers among the mountain, and when I past on all mountains and rivers and lakes, then I came to a great plain. I did not saw any trees or any hills, just a very good green grass and all kinds of flowers. Then I dropped into a small trail, then I went into it and I follow all along, said he. Then someone asked, How long you went then you reach the great plain? Then he answers, Almost fifteen days. Then continue the man, I don't see the end of this great plain. Then when I reach in the center I saw a smoke ascented a little distance yonder, so I walked quickly as I could. Soon I arrived at the brim of the large pit and I looked down. I saw a hut stood down the bottom to where the smoke ascented. Therefore I went down by the same small trail and I went down the hill quickly with my rifle on my shoulder. So when I reached down the bottom of a valley, I went towards the hut. I look in secretly. That the large man lay along

side the fire with his back against the fire, which said to me, Come in sir, for I already saw thee struggling all along the way. So I went in quietly, and I sat on one side of his fire with my rifle at my front. There his sat up, a great man look at me with his large rough face, and I was afraid to him. He said that if I not afraid to see him, so I took my courage. Then he asked me if I knew him. Then I say no. Continues asking me if I knew the history about Tkamshim and I say yes. Then he told me that he is him. He was Tkamshim. Also he told me and saw me a big wound at his breast that he received in the house of one chief named Dhamnunk. Carving the interior they shot me, says he. I see two little pups lying sleeping around the fire. Then the giant told me the almighty placed him there in the bottom of the pit and nourished him there, so he won't go round the country. Then he fed me a good food, and when I finished he asked me to go outside his house. So I did as he told me. We forth, and he point me the tops of all them mountains round about his hut. All them mountains were full with all kinds of animals, mountain sheeps, Black Bears, and so on. Then he asked me again if I want to go back to my home. Therefore I told him that I don't know my way. Further more told him how hardly to get home again. Then he smile and said is not very far from here, said he. You reach home tonight. I will give you victuals on the way and you home. So I agree to what he said. Moreover he told me that the almighty give him two dogs, while he call them two little pups, who come forth and shaking their bodies they became young Lions. Now I am almost faint. They went up to where the numerable mountain sheep were. Soon they went behold the great number of mountain sheeps slidding down on the side of a mountain. So Tkamshim cuts them all off flesh and also fats. Therefore he put them meats and fats on this cane these you ate now. And while he give this cane to me, and he point to me a small trail. It reached behind your home, and stretched out his hand over the plain. He done it four times. And he commanded me if I not look behind if I hear a awful noise or else if you look back some danger came to you on the way and you will not get home, or if you look straight ahead you get home tonight. After he had command me, I went and I ran with all might, with cane on my right hand and my rifle on my left shoulder. While ran I heard behind me a great terrible noise behind me as a thunder rolling, which makes me much afraid. So I ran. Then more noise awful and fearful right close my back and shakes all the ground, noise as the rocks rents. I went on. More noise tremble almost fails me, and all them noise more exceeding terrible. Yet I am almost out of breath, and before evening dawn I've arrive at this top of this hill above us, and I layed my cane and my rifle. Soon as I reached above the hill behind this village I'll look back the way I come from. Behold I saw many mountains' tops on the way I came from. I wonder. I thought I was a dream, till I come down, and when I saw my sister weeping there I perceived it was sure.

And all his people was glad to see him home again. All his relation gladly welcome him once more. And now he kept the cane that Tkamshim gave it to him. So the people knew that Tkamshim his still alive now.

My cousin Mr. Henry D. Pierce[4] *met the man last summer and my cousin asked him, and the man told him all these stories that I put down on these pages now. And all the people knew it now, and many young people tried to find him, but they won't. Tkamshim hide himself among the mountains so the people cannot found him.*

Notes

1 "Gilauzui tribe": the Gilodza or Gilutsau, the Lakelse Band of Lakelse (Kaxgels) River, near Terrace, B.C. In a close re-telling of this narrative to William Beynon in 1954, Dan Goswell of the Gilodza tribe claimed this as a crest story: "Inside the house Temnunx related the narrative of the young man. It was then proclaimed to all that Wiget was the exclusive property of the house of Temnunx, and this was affirmed by all the guests" (Cove and MacDonald 1987:46).

2 "Not many years ago": The establishment of the first cannery on the Skeena was in 1877—see Seguin, ed. 1984:47.

3 "Lions": Tate's Tsimshian word is "houhout," which Boas prints as *hauhau*, and glosses as "a fabulous animal" (1916:102).

4 "Henry D. Pierce": Henry Pierce was later an informant for William Beynon. His version of the origin of Raven exists in manuscript, but apparently he did not pass on this sequel about the Raven being alive. Beynon wrote a note to Boas in a manuscript of about 1935-36: "My informant had assisted Henry Tate in his mss. for you," adding that Pierce "has always been a studious man...He is much more intelligent than the average and in age is about 70 years."

Sucking-Intestines

This may or may not count as a Raven story, depending upon whom you believe. Boas heard it as a Raven origin story from Mrs. Lawson, a Tsimshian living in Victoria at the time of his first visit to the Pacific coast in 1886. When Tate came up with an entirely different birth for Raven (see "Origin of Raven," above), Boas was perturbed, and paraphrased Mrs. Lawson's version in a letter of 22 May 1905 to try to jog Tate's memory. Tate replied that this "SuckingIntestines" story was "different altogether," not part of the Raven cycle (letter to Boas, 6 July 1905). There is reason to believe that Tate was right and that the story derives from a French fabliaux brought in by fur traders. Boas wanted it anyway, and asked for it specifically in letters of 19 December 1906, 28 March 1907, and 29 August 1907. Tate gave in, and finally sat down, again with *Tsimshian Texts* (1902) as authority, to compose something on demand. Amazingly, it turned out to be one of his finest pieces.

Tate really enjoys embellishing his source here, and creates an entirely new ending, of some symbolic power. The spruce tree which was the boy's birthplace and the scene of his mother's adultery, burns and licks him up with its flame.

There is no escaping the rather disagreeable title, "Sucking-Intestines." It is a direct translation of the protagonist's Tsimshian name. Boas used it as the title of the story in *Tsimshian Mythology* (1916:214).

◆

The History of sucked the Intestine

There was a great town at Metlakahtla
   the village of Gishbakloush[1]
      call Red bear Village
         in which a great chief and chieftainess
            and also the chief's nephew
               were living.

The young man
   fell in lover
      to the chieftainess
         which she love him most,
            but the chief
               did not know it.

The young man often
   went in to her
      and lied down with her
         while the chief was away.
            Then she became
               to be pregnant.

Then the chieftainess resolved
   I will pretend to die
      on your behalf
         so they all agreed.

So on the next day the chieftainess pretended to be very sick, because she love the young man better than her husband and she wanted to marry that young man. Not many days since her sickness she said to her old husband,

When I die you might bury me in a
large box. Do not burn my body.
Just put my horn spoon in my coffin,
and my marten's garment and also
my fish knife.

After a short time
she pretended to die.
Then all the chief's tribe gather
and cried for her.

So the people make a large box to bury her. They put her into
it, with two marten blankets and one sea-otter garment, also many
dozen goodly horn spoon, with fish knife, and they put it on the
tree at the little Island at the front of the Village.
Now she pretended
to be dead.

After two nights
that the chief
went over
the little Island,
and sat
right under the coffin
into which the chieftainess
was lying.

His weeping.

Then while he was there
he beheld grubs
falling down
from the chieftainess' coffin.
Then the chief thought
she is full of grubs
so he make him
wept bitterly.

(But the chieftainess actually scraping the spoon horn with her fish knife into the coffin, so the scraping the horn spoon lookeds just like as maggots.)

And since the chieftainess was in her coffin, that the young man went into her every night, in her coffin, while the village people was all slept. He went over the little Island, and he climbed on the tree and kicked the cover of the coffin saying,
Let me in to you, ghost.
Then the chieftainess was laugh in her coffin bed,
Ha ha-ay
in your behalf
I pretended
to make grubs
myself.
So she opened her coffin cover and the man went in and lay down with her. The young man always went up to her every night. But the great chief did not know it. He still weeping, no one could comfort him.

The other night some another young people went over that little Island where the chieftainess layed. They soon sats with his sweetheart under the chieftainess' coffin. They behold a young man coming over to where they was.
They knew it was the chief's nephew.
He climbed up to where the chieftainess' coffin, he kick the coffin cover, he says, Let me in to you, ghost. Then they heard the chieftainess was laughing in her coffin. They heard her replied, Ha ha-ay, I pretended to make maggots of myself in your behalf. They saw the young man went into her coffin,
and this young couple
heard that was played
in the coffin.
Then before the day light
that the nephew of the chief
come out from the coffin.

Then they told it to the chief.

So the chief send over his two attendants to kept watch the chieftainess' coffin, and he commanded them, If it is sure, throw down the coffin. Therefore these two attendants went over. They watch the coffin, and while village people was sleep they behold a man coming over. They knew it was the chief's nephew. He climbed up the tree to where chieftainess layed. Soon as he reached the top the coffin, he kicked the coffin cover, saying,

Let me in to you, ghost.

They heard chieftainess laughing. She replied,

Ha ha-ay
I pretended
to make maggots
out of
your behalf.

These attendants heard
their was played
in the coffin
and at midnight
they heard
their was ceased.

These attendants knew their was slept, therefore they climbed on the tree and they threw down the large coffin.
The chieftainess was bursted
and the chief's nephew also was killed.

And when these men come down
they saw a baby boy
was among the intestines
of his mother.

They went into the chief's house. They told him it was true. They told him also that the child was alive. Then the chief order them to bring the child to him, so they brought the child to him.

It sucked the intestines of its mother.
Therefore the child name was "Sucking-Intestines."

Then the chief take one of good female slave to be his nurse.

The child grew up in chief's house, and the chief love the little boy most. And when the boy was able to walk, he went over often to that little Island to get Spruce chewing-gum, for he likes chewing-gum best at the same Spruce where his mother's coffin was on while she pretended to make maggots out of herself. And the chief took him over and burnt him some pitch with fire to let the child chewing. With some of his slaves they did it so many time.

> The boy walked over
> > alone to that Island
> > > and get gum   out of the same Spruce
> > > > to his mother's grave.

> His mind was set
> > on the little Island
> > > to where his born.

He played around the Island   almost every day   so the slaves took him over there.

He became a beautiful young boy. Now the chief love him more every day. Therefore on the next day that the young boy said to his father (the chief), Let us go over to that little Island and burnt off the pitch with fire. So the chief went with him, and some of his slaves. Then the chief order his male slave to burnt off the pitch. So they did. They burnt pitch. Then the chief sat near the Spruce with the boy stood at the front of him.

> > Then the flamed of the fire
> > > like a tongue
> > > > took the boy
> > > > > from the chief's bosom.
> > And the boy was burnt to dead,
> > > and the chief was moarned again.
> > > > For the fire swallowed up the boy.

Now this is the end of "Sucking-Intestines." Now we call this little Island "She-Pretended-To-Make-Grubs."[2]

Notes

1 "Gishbakloush": Gispaxloats, a tribal group of the Tsimshian. "In the course of migrations from the Skeena River to the coast the local groups maintained their tribal identity...Thus the town known as Old Metlakatla actually consists of dwellings each of which is identified by the name of the tribe inhabiting it. Most of the tribes occupied several clusters of dwellings or villages" (Garfield 1939:175). "Red bear village" would be just one of several Gispaxloats locations. Tate's Tsimshian name for it, "Lakmishaula," is a place-name found as "Lexmesola" on the map "Winter Villages Around Prince Rupert Harbour" in Cove and MacDonald 1987:xiii.

2 "She-Pretended-To-Make-Grubs": Tate's Tsimshian name for the island is "Lakshishtaksha'andh." It has not been identified, but it could be the present-day Anian Island.

Bibliography

Barbeau, C. Marius
1928 *The Downfall of Temlaham* (Edmonton: Hurtig Publishers, reprint 1973)
1929 *Totem Poles of the Gitksan* (Ottawa: National Museum of Canada, Anthropological Series 12.61, reprint 1978)
1950 *Totem Poles* 2 vols. (Ottawa: National Museum of Canada Anthropological Series 30.119, reprint 1973)
1953 *Haida Myths Illustrated in Argillite Carvings* (Ottawa: National Museum of Canada, Anthropological Series 32.127)
1961 *Tsimsyan Myths* (Ottawa: National Museum of Canada, Anthropological Series 51.174)

Boas, Franz
1902 *Tsimshian Texts* (Washington: Bureau of American Ethnology Bulletin 27)
1912 *Tsimshian Texts (New Series)* (Leyden: E.J. Brill for the American Ethnological Society Publications Vol. 3)
1916 *Tsimshian Mythology* (Washington: Bureau of American Ethnology, 31st Annual Report)

Cove, John
1987 *Shattered Images: Dialogues and Meditations on Tsimshian Narratives* (Ottawa: Carleton Univ. Press)

Cove, John, and George F. MacDonald
1987 *Tsimshian Narratives* 2 vols. (Ottawa: Canadian Museum of Civilization, Mercury Series, Directorate Paper 3)

Dalzell, Kathleen E.
1973 *The Queen Charlotte Islands Book 2: Of Places and Names* (Prince Rupert, B.C.: Dalzell Books)

de Laguna, Frederica
1972 *Under Mount Saint Elias: The History and Culture of the Yakutat Tlingit* (Washington: Smithsonian Contributions to Anthropology 7)

Dunn, John Asher
1978 *A Practical Dictionary of the Coast Tsimshian Language* (Ottawa: National Museums of Canada, Canadian Ethnology Service Paper 42)

Garfield, Viola
1939   *Tsimshian Clan and Society* (Seattle: Univ. of Washington Publications in Anthropology 7.3)

Halpin, Marjorie
1973   *The Tsimshian Crest System* (Ph.D.dissertation, University of British Columbia, Vancouver)

Jacobs, Melville
1959   *The Content and Style of an Oral Literature* (Chicago: Univ. of Chicago Press)

McClellan, Catherine
1970   *The Girl Who Married the Bear* (Ottawa: National Museum of Man, Publications in Ethnology 2)
1975   *My Old People Say* (Ottawa: National Museum of Man, Publications in Ethnology 6)

Miller, Jay, and Carol M. Eastman
1984   *The Tsimshian and Their Neighbors of the North Pacific Coast* (Seattle: Univ. of Washington Press)

Seguin, Margaret
1984   *The Tsimshian* (Vancouver: Univ. of British Columbia Press)

Thompson, Stith
1929   *Tales of the North American Indians* (Bloomington: Indiana Univ. Press)